$22⁹⁵

An
Identification & Value Guide To

THIRD EDITION
DEPRESSION ERA
GLASSWARE

DEDICATION

To Ann and Freeman,
two extraordinary people I love dearly
and who believe in me with the passions of the soul and -
of the mind.

CONTENTS

DEPRESSION GLASS
Key For Cover Photos

GREEN	TOPAZ or YELLOW	ULTRAMARINE	AMBER (Light)
CREMAX	FOREST GREEN	PINK	FROSTED or PINK SATIN FINISH
PINK (Orange Cast)	MONAX	COBALT	GREEN OPALESCENT

FRONT COVER

BACK COVER

CRYSTAL	RUBY RED	CRYSTAL on METAL BASE	IRIDESCENT
JADITE	LIGHT BLUE	DELPHITE	AMETHYST
SHELL PINK	AMBER (Dark)	OPALESCENT	IRIDESCENT

INTRODUCTION TO THE SECOND EDITION

I have been writing books on collecting for many years now and had a great deal of fun and gained much satisfaction derivative of the required travels and the people I have spent much time with in the pursuit of information. I did not have to travel far for this one for through happenstance I met a lady with a fine collection of glassware of the depression era who had her shop a mere seventeen miles from my front door. Her name is Mary Burris and her shop, Mary B's Antiques. As you may note, her name appears with mine on the cover and title page. Yes, I wrote the book but it would not have been possible to do so without Mary Burris. Over the first months and now years Mary became indispensable as a consultant and seemingly bottomless source of glassware for the pattern drawings in this book.

We had many discussions about how the information in this book should be presented. She and I along with the publisher finally hit upon a concept entirely new to the guide books in depression era glassware collecting. I am sure you have already noticed this departure from the norm, the presentation of pattern design in drawing form rather than pattern identification data. Photography in other books varies from quite poor black and white to strikingly beautiful full color plates, but often does not show subtle identifying design details.

The book is admittedly incomplete even with the addition of many new patterns in since the first edition. In the first place there has never and never will be a complete collectors' guide in this particular collecting discipline. There is too much not known as yet, but the overruling reason is that even the experts disagree frequently on just what is or is not properly labeled "Depression Era Glass" and collectible as such.

Secondly, this book is meant not only to be a useful reference to those who already collect, but to provide the new or beginning collector with a simple, easy-to-use tool for learning. To do more would probably quadruple the size not to mention the price of the book.

There are literally millions of collectors of depression era glassware. There are myraid dealers, numerous shows from local to national and, fortunately, much glassware to satisfy the appetites of all these people. Most patterns are inexpensive to accumulate and available in quantity.

There are at least one hundred formal organizations, two national publications and several books devoted to the hobby.

Friends and acquaintances of mine frequently ask what I am working on at the time. When I answered the questions questions with "A book on depression glass", I was almost always met with comments such as "What is that?", "That doesn't sound very interesting." Boy, are they mistaken! They just don't know what I have found out in the course of my research. I'm here to tell you that they don't know about the beauty of design and the excitement of color that characterizes "that old cheap dimestore glass that came in oatmeal boxes or flour sacks." I suppose some of them might recall "glass night" at the neighborhood movie house. With the purchase of your ticket came a piece of glassware and when the movie was over and house lights came on, with it came the crash of glass from every direction as people stood up, forgetting what was in their laps. That crash was the sound signifying what was to become one of the most popular collecting hobbies in the United States today.

What follows here is an introduction to that hobby and a guide to its pursuit.

Mary Burris
Special Consultant to **Depression Era Glass for Collectors**

Mary Burris was absolutely indispensable to me in the preparation of the manuscript for this book. We spent many hours together in her shop, with me the student and Mary the teacher, in between customers.

She, like all the other depression glass collectors I have met, became very animated and bubbling over when I began asking the normal questions about how long she had been collecting, how it got started, and so forth. This enthusiasm seems to be a very common trait among depression glass collectors.

Mary has been, along with her husband incidentally, collecting it for well over thirty five years. She said she became a dealer out of self-defense. "There were so many boxes under the beds I couldn't clean under them without darn near breaking my back and we got awfully worried about all the weight of the boxes in the attic. We didn't want to be killed in a glass avalanche so I became a dealer."

What she kept at home is a magnificent collection of about 500 pieces but what will really interest the collector is her shop. "Mary B's Antiques" stocks literally thousands and thousands of pieces of depression glass. It has been said that she has one of the largest selections in the south.

She has an enormous storehouse of knowledge regarding the glass and enthusiastically shares it with her customers.

In my past books I have usually encouraged collectors to write me direct when they have questions or news of new discoveries. In this case Mary is better qualified than I am to field these questions and she has graciously offered to do so in my stead.

Now I must ask you to be very selective as to what you contact her about. I have many books in print presently and each one of them generates more correspondence than I can realistically handle. Mary will do her best to answer your questions I know, but don't forget that she has to run a business. It is for this reason that I strongly suggest that you do not telephone her at all and do remember to include a stamped, self-addressed envelope when writing. She's a heckofa nice gal, but she ain't Superwoman.

MARY B's ANTIQUES
P. O. Box 158
Rogersville, Alabama 35652

If you are traveling north or south on Interstate 65 you should make sure you allow time for a side trip to Mary B's Antiques. It is only a 30 minute trip to Rogersville on Highway 72 West from I-65. You get off the interstate at the Athens, Alabama, exit. The shop is presently open Monday through Saturday, but it might be best to call first.

If it possible for you to visit the shop, I can guarantee you're likely to find just what you've been looking for. If you wish to stay overnight there is a nice motel a very short distance away. In addition there is a wonderful state park and lodge just outside Rogersville on Wheeler lake with a modern hotel, restaurant, swimming beach, marina with boat rental, hiking trails and a state-of-the-art campground with all amenities, including a store, for your camper or motor home. Anybody in town can direct you there. Just a short thirty minutes further west on Highway 72 puts you in the world famous Muscle Shoals Area or Florence, Sheffield, Tuscumbia and the town of Muscle Shoals. There are plenty of shopping, dining and entertainment opportunities available here. Among other things the Shoals Area is home to the Helen Keller Home, the W.C. Handy, Father of the Blues home and Wilson Dam where you can visit the water turbine hydro electric generation powerhouse and the world's highest single-lift navigation lock. If I sound like a commercial then so be it. It's my home and I'm proud of it.

Carl Luckey

DEPRESSION GLASS

There is a book available that curiously predicts that depression glass among other things is a collectible of tomorrow. The author is sadly mistaken. It is a collectible of today, most assuredly.

Depression glass came into being in the 1920's and what we call depression glass is more accurately labelled depression era glass. It is glassware made from just a few years before the Great Depression through and on into the 1940's*. Most of it is characterized by a machine-molded design incorporating design patterns that are often very intricately detailed, but also occur in optic and/or geometric motifs.

The colors used are another very distinctive characteristic of this glassware. The product was manufactured to be cheap, frequently on order to be given away as advertising or promotional premiums. Some have even said the colors were used to disguise what would otherwise appear to be imperfect, bubbled and streaked glass. Whether this is true is open to argument. Whatever the reasons, the colors used are distinctive and at times striking in intensity and depth. Most characteristically it is found in varying transparent hues of pink, green, blue, yellow, or clear glass with no color at all, referred to as "crystal" by dealers and collectors. There were of course many other colors used, but those listed above are the most common. The items depicted in color on the cover of this book were selected to give you a representation of the majority of colors that you may find.

*Some glassware included in the broad category of depression glass is still being produced. This will be discussed later.

* ABOUT THE VALUES IN THIS BOOK *

You will immediately note, upon looking at the pattern listings, that the values of the items listed is presented in ranges. This is a more realistic approach to valuation, because that is what you will run into when buying. Values can vary greatly from dealer to dealer and region to region.

The values given are here and now, at the time this book is being written, and will represent an opinion derived from today's market and many years of dealer experience. The value ranges are a **guide,** nothing more.

Values such as presented in this book are useful only when used in conjunction with several other value guides, price lists, etc., and the experience level of the user. People have a tendency to jump right into price lists upon obtaining books such as this, with no regard to the introductory material, and to use these value guides as the final word, their value Bible as it were. They select this or any other guide as a quick and final answer. The people who use the guides most effectively are those who view them only as one of the four or five other factors that should be considered in each specific instance where one needs to evaluate an item for sale or purchase.

RESTORATION OR REPAIR

Condition of pieces is a factor influencing value. If a particular item is badly scratched and chipped, it will very likely fall far below the lower figure in the value range for it.

If an item has only small or one or two chips or scratches, it can be fairly easily repaired by a competent craftsman specializing in this type of work. These people can also repair broken stems and such. Many times the repairs are flawless and undetectable.

Because of the relative abundance of many patterns and the requirement of only a small outlay for most, I don't consider well-repaired or restored items as worthless or worth less than the same non-damaged item. Ethically, however, those that have been repaired should always be presented as such.

One last word: It may be cheaper just to buy a replacement, if you can find it. In the case of repairs, look before you leap.

REISSUES, REPRODUCTIONS AND FAKES

Fortunately, depression era glassware is, in the main, an inexpensive collectible. There are, however, a few exceptions. To see an extraordinary exception one only has to turn to the Mayfair ("Open Rose") pattern by Hocking and look over the figures in the value listing.

If you have looked at the pages mentioned above and recovered sufficiently from the shock, I will try to relieve your mind by reiterating: Collecting depression glass is an inexpensive hobby if you shop wisely and employ at least a modicum of patience.

Now, in view of the lofty prices of the "Open Rose" pattern, we must discuss an ugly problem. In any area of collecting, when some of the items are rare and/or avidly sought, there are some who will attempt to take advantage of it. There are several different ways to profit by the popularity or rarity of various patterns and specific items of depression glass. These run the full spectrum from honest profit motives to downright dishonesty.

As you read through the pattern discussions you will come across a few (very few) instances where the company that originated the pattern in the 1920's or 1930's is still in business and is either still producing it or, worse, **has reissued the old pattern using the original molds.** That this is a matter of their prerogative and that it is quite honest is a foregone conclusion. After all, they own the design and molds. My argument with this is not new or original but it is nonetheless valid. I join the ranks of the others in objecting to this practice as a disservice to collectors and, indirectly, to the very companies doing it. The company is in the business of making money, of course, and taking advantage of a potentially profitable market situation, by definition makes money. What the companies don't realize is the very real presence of another market situation; the **millions** of consumers who collect depression glass. To illustrate this, suppose the original company were to reissue the entire line of the above-mentioned expensive pattern. That would not only make the collectors of that pattern hopping mad, but the event would make headlines across the country in all the collector publications. Now that represents bad media exposure to millions of people. If that wouldn't drive the company's public relations director to the brink, I don't know what would. Now the solution to the dilemma of reissues is a simple one and I wonder that it is not often used. All the reissuing company has to do is mark the items in such a way as to make it obvious that it is indeed a reissue; placing a date or mark in the mold to make the reissue easy to spot.

The scenario painted above is admittedly extreme, but clearly the practice of reissuing has to have some impact on the company, however small.

Jumping to the other end of the spectrum we find ourselves face to face with that nefarious character, the crook. This vulture in the blue sky of collecting can swoop down on you in several forms; the dishonest dealer, the thief, the deceiver and the faker or forger. The dishonest dealer is fairly rare, but the crook in concert (knowingly or unknowingly) with the forger is a clear and present danger.

A recent collector periodical carried an article about a lady showing up at a show with a "family heirloom." She went from dealer to dealer carrying a "Miss America" butter dish (value range: $188 to $425 depending upon color) offering it for sale. Some bit and bought, others balked. It was a reproduction or a fake. I don't presume to judge whether it was an intentional fake or a legitimate (?) reproduction, but that the woman was a thief there can be no doubt.

The balking dealers knew their stuff and so must you. You have to study, learn and experience your hobby.

There have been just a few of these reproductions or fakes to show up so far and they are listed and described in detail in this book for you. They are discussed with each pattern in which they occur.

There are many other items of depression glass that could be attractive to interested shady individuals, so arm yourself with knowledge.

PATTERN LISTING

The following section is the pattern identification guide. It is arranged alphabetically according to the pattern name most often used; either official company nomenclature or in the absence of that, the name given and used most often by collectors.

Under each listing you will find the company that produced the pattern, the colors that you might find in the pattern and a description of the pattern, some history and rarities to be found.

When there are reproductions or reissues known, they are discussed as well.

The last category to appear with each listing is the pattern value range chart.

PATTERN INDEX

Following is an alphabetical listing of all pattern names or nicknames that are or have been used to facilitate ease of location. For example, if you are in the habit of calling "Cameo" by the name "Ballerina" or "Dancing Girl", you will find it listed all three ways in the index.

PATTERN INDEX

ADAM

1932 - 1934

Jeannette Glass Company   Jeannette, Pennsylvania

Colors found to date:

- Crystal
  - Topaz (rare)
- Green
- Yellow (very rare)
- Pink

Reproductions or Reissues   ADAM

So far there is only one piece in the Adam line that is known to have been reproduced. The covered butter dish in pink only has been offered by the A. A. Importing Co., Inc. It is 6 inches across and the only way to really tell the new from the old is to be familiar with the look of genuine Depression Era pink. The new piece has a pink color that has a decidedly "washed out" or "watery" look in comparison.

General Pattern Notes

Sometimes the collector may encounter the factory trademark of a "J" enclosed in a triangle but this occurs so infrequently it is an unreliable indicator.

The color most commonly found in the Adam pattern is pink. It is also the most popularly collected color.

Variations to look for are the pitchers found with both round and square bases; butter dishes whose lids are found with the Adam pattern or a combination of the Adam with the Sierra pattern on the lids. The latter variation is found only in pink so far. The Sierra design is on the outside and the Adam design is on the inside.

Candy and sugar lids are identical.

ITEM	DESCRIPTION & REMARKS	DOLLAR VALUE RANGES BY COLOR	
		Pink	Green
Ash tray	4½"	27-33	25-31
Bowl	4¾"	17-19	15-18
Bowl	5¾"	27-33	22-28
Bowl	7¾"	30-35	35-40
Bowl (covered)	9"	48-57	85-100
Bowl (oval)	10"	20-25	27-33
Butter dish and cover		90-110	300-410
Butter dish (combination "Sierra" pattern)		575-725	—
Cake plate (footed)	10"	17-22	25-30
Candlesticks (pair)	4"	70-83	100-112
Candy jar and cover		75-90	95-115
Coaster	3¼"	20-27	18-22
Creamer		14-19	18-22
Cup		20-29	24-32
Lamp		225-250	240-260
Pitcher	8"	37-44	44-52
Pitcher (round base)	32 oz.	41-53	—
Plate	6"	7-9	7-10
Plate (square)	7¾"	12-14	12-15
Plate (square)	9"	20-25	20-31
Plate (grill)	9"	18-21	16-20
Platter	11¾"	14-18	21-26
Relish dish (sectioned)	8"	13-16	14-19
Salt & Pepper (footed)	4"	60-76	90-126
Saucer (square)	6"	5-8	5-9
Sherbet		17-20	25-30
Sugar		12-16	18-22
Sugar or Candy Cover		19-25	27-34
Tumbler	4½"	26-31	20-31
Tumbler	5½"	40-48	37-44
Vase	7½"	190-220	42-54

AMERICAN PIONEER

1931 - 1934

Liberty Works   Egg Harbor, New Jersey

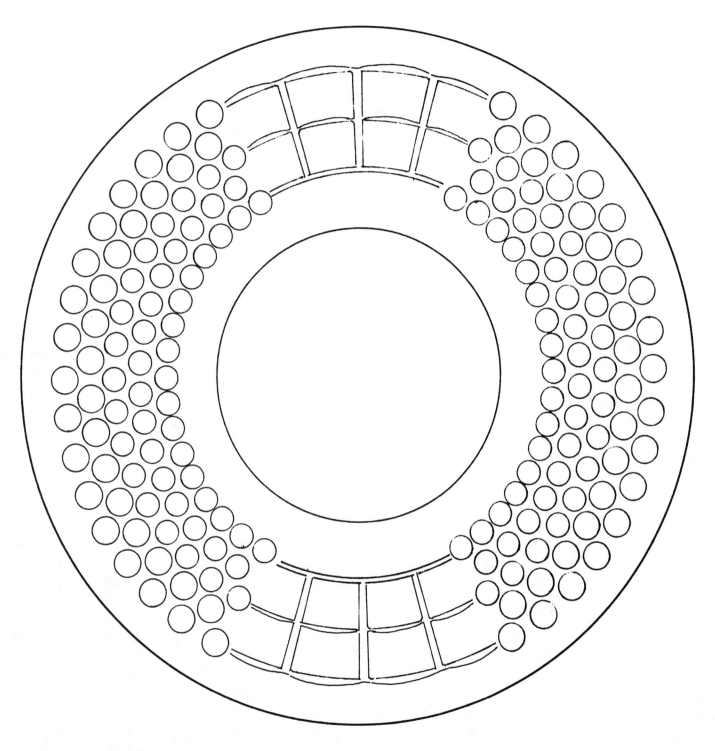

Colors found to date:
- Amber
- Crystal
- Green
- Pink

Reproductions or Reissues
None are known.

General Pattern Notes

This is one of the more uncommon patterns as can be readily seen by some of the values listed below. Early Liberty Works advertisements state: "Each piece will carry an embossed paper label worded 'American Pioneer,' by Liberty'", but these are seldom seen. About the only way the collector might find a piece with the label intact would be if he were fortunate enough to stumble upon some unsold boxed stock in a dark and dusty corner.

Green is the most popularly collected color followed quite closely by pink. Amber is the rare color and crystal follows far behind pink and green in popularity.

Rare pieces are the whiskey jigger and the post-Prohibition 3 ounce wine goblets. Also difficult to locate are the 8 ounce water goblets and the two sizes of covered bowls.

ITEM	DESCRIPTION & REMARKS	DOLLAR VALUE RANGES BY COLOR		
		Crystal	Green	Pink
Bowl	5" (handled)	11-13	13-17	12-14
Bowl	8¾" (covered)	78-95	94-105	79-95
Bowl	9" (handled)	14-17	21-29	14-17
Bowl	9¼" (covered)	92-107	121-160	92-106
Bowl	10 3/8" (console)	48-65	65-82	48-65
Candlesticks 6½" (pair)		65-75	83-102	65-75
Candy Jar and cover (small)		63-74	76-90	63-74
Candy jar and cover (large)		79-99	92-100	79-99
Cheese and cracker set (indented plate and compote)		22-29	26-33	22-29
Coaster	3½"	19-22	24-30	19-22
Creamer	(small)	10-11	11-14	10-11
Creamer	(large)	9-10	11-14	9-10
Cup		5-9	10-14	5-9
Dresser Set	(2 colognes, powder jar, 7½" tray)	85-143	—	85-143
Goblet	4"	19-22	27-33	19-22
Goblet	6"	22-29	27-32	22-29
Ice Bucket	6"	26-31	43-52	26-31
Lamp	(ball shaped) (amber: 55-77)	71-90	—	71-90
Lamp	8½"	79-98	99-112	79-98
Pitcher	5" (covered) (amber: 250-330)	108-142	180-205	108-142
Pitcher	7" (covered) (amber: 250-330)	140-170	190-216	140-170
Plate	8"	5-9	5-8	5-9
Plate	11½" (handled)	13-17	18-22	13-17
Saucer		2-4	8-9	2-4
Sherbet	3½"	9-10	13-17	9-10
Sherbet	4¾"	14-16	19-22	14-16
Sugar	2¾"	7-9	10-12	7-9
Sugar	3½"	9-10	12-14	9-10
Tumbler	5 oz.	14-18	21-29	14-18
Tumbler	4"	19-22	26-32	19-22
Tumbler	5"	22-29	43-51	22-29
Vase	4¼" (footed rose bowl)	55-65	82-98	55-65
Vase	7" (4 styles)	84-95	102-128	84-95
Whiskey Jigger 2¼"		44-52	48-59	44-52

AMERICAN SWEETHEART

1930 - 1936

Macbeth-Evans Glass Company   Charleroi, Pennsylvania

Colors found to date:

- Cremax
- Pink
- Dark Blue
- Ruby red
- Monax
- Smoke

Reproductions or Reissues

None are known.

General Pattern Notes

American Sweetheart is probably one of the most popular of the Macbeth-Evans pattern lines. The name was given the pattern by collectors as the company referred to it as its "R Pattern". It originally appeared in pink but soon became available in the other colors. The monax pieces are sometimes found with colored rims, and the very rare smoke is always found black-rimmed.

The patterns are found both on the front and reverse sides and sometimes a combination of sides. Sometimes on the monax pieces the center portion of the design is omitted altogether. Incidentally, if you find a gold-rimmed Monax piece, it is dated 1935 or later. That year is when they added the gold rim. Pitchers and tumblers have so far been found in pink only.

Pitchers and salt/pepper shakers are the most difficult pieces to find in this pattern.

This is one of the very few patterns that presents sherbets with no stem or base. The sherbets are made to fit into a metal base.

ITEM	DESCRIPTION & REMARKS	DOLLAR VALUE RANGES BY COLOR					
		Cremax	Monax	Blue	Pink	Red	Smoke
Bowl	3¾"	—	—	—	33-39	—	—
Bowl	4½" cream soup	—	57-70	—	30-35	—	—
Bowl	6"	12-15	16-19	—	12-15	—	37-44
Bowl	9" (round)	46-56	55-65	—	22-26	—	95-109
Bowl	9½" (flat soup)	—	57-70	—	33-38	—	—
Bowl	11" (oval)	—	62-73	—	39-45	—	—
Bowl	18" (console)	—	480-620	950-1200	—	950-1200	—
Creamer	(footed)	—	12-16	143-168	11-13	125-145	68-83
Cup		—	14-18	143-168	14-17	125-145	68-78
Lampshade		630-655	685-815	—	—	—	—
Plate	6"	—	5-8	—	3-6	—	22-26
Plate	8"	—	11-15	132-162	8-11	110-125	36-41
Plate	9"	—	13-17	—	—	—	46-53
Plate	9¾"	—	22-26	—	22-26	—	68-83
Plate	10¼"	—	22-28	—	22-26	—	—
Plate	11"	—	17-22	—	—	—	—
Plate	12" (salver)	—	17-22	295-345	14-18	209-239	—
Plate	15½"	—	275-300	418-508	—	405-493	—
Platter	13" (oval)	—	57-71	—	22-27	—	120-142
Pitcher	7½"	—	—	—	500-570	—	—
Pitcher	8"	—	—	—	408-448	—	—
Salt and Pepper (footed)		—	340-390	—	440-490	—	—
Saucer		—	4-7	55-65	3-6	45-57	22-26
Sherbet	4" (footed)	—	—	—	17-20	—	—
Sherbet	4¼" (footed)	—	22-28	—	13-17	—	41-50
Sherbet in Metal Holder (crystal only: 5-9)		—	—	—	—	—	—
Sugar	(footed, no cover)	—	11-17	150-174	11-14	125-145	70-80
Sugar cover	(monax only)	—	275-300	—	—	—	—
Tid Bit	(3 level, 8", 12", 15½")	—	220-260	825-925	—	660-735	—
Tumbler	3½"	—	—	—	50-55	—	—
Tumbler	4"	—	—	—	50-55	—	—
Tumbler	4½"	—	—	—	65-70	—	—

ANNIVERSARY
1947 - 1949

Jeannette Glass Company

Jeannette, Pennsylvania

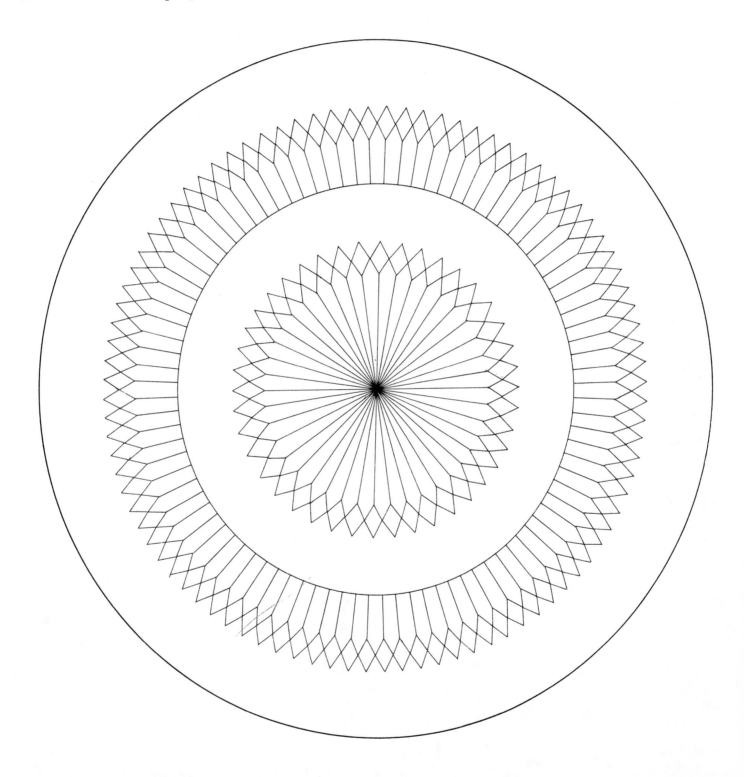

Colors found to date:

- Amethyst (odd pieces)
- Pink

- Crystal*
- White (odd pieces)

- Iridescent

*Crystal may be found with a gold or silver rim.

Reproductions or Reissues
    None are known.

General Pattern Notes
    Strictly speaking the 1947-49 date is inaccurate. Jeannette began producing the pattern in pink only in those years but they made Anniversary in the crystal and iridescent right up into the 1970's. Most collectors do not seriously consider these two colors part of depression glass collecting. The value listing below contains only those items that were in the 1947 pattern produced in pink.

ITEM	DESCRIPTION & REMARKS	DOLLAR VALUE RANGES BY COLOR
		Pink
Bowl	4 7/8"	3-6
Bowl	7 3/8"	9-11
Bowl	9"	15-20
Butter dish and cover		60-71
Candy jar and cover		37-45
Compote	(3 legged)	10-12
Cake Plate	12½"	11-14
Cover	(for cake plate)	19-22
Creamer (footed)		9-11
Cup		5-8
Pickle Dish	9"	8-10
Plate	6¼"	3-6
Plate	9"	8-11
Plate	12½"	10-13
Relish Dish	8"	10-13
Saucer		2-5
Sherbet	(footed)	5-9
Sugar and cover		14-19
Vase	6½"	13-18
Wall Vase		18-22
Wine Glass		12-17

AUNT POLLY

c. 1920

U. S. Glass Company

*Pittsburgh, Pennsylvania

Colors found to date:

- Blue
- Green
- Iridescent (amber)

* The company had numerous locations for factories. Pittsburgh was one of the only two factories still operating in 1938.

Reproductions or Reissues
    None found to date.

General Pattern Notes
    For many years the manufacturer of this pattern was not known but recently catalog evidence was found that identifies the U. S. Glass Company as its maker.
    Rarest of the pattern are the salt and pepper shakers, oval bowls, and sugars with cover.

ITEM	DESCRIPTION & REMARKS	DOLLAR VALUE RANGES BY COLOR	
		Blue	Green & Iridescent
Bowl	4 3/8"	6-10	6-9
Bowl	4¾"	18-22	13-18
Bowl	7¼" (oval, handled)	18-22	13-18
Bowl	7 7/8"	25-29	15-20
Bowl	8 3/8" (oval)	37-44	29-33
Butter Dish and cover		195-235	210-245
Creamer		32-39	24-30
Pitcher	8"	150-175	—
Plate	6"	5-9	4-6
Plate	8"	11-13	—
Salt and Pepper shakers (pair)		265-310	—
Sherbet		12-14	12-14
Sugar and cover		80-105	65-73
Tumbler	8 oz.	19-23	—
Vase	6½" (footed)	40-60	33-39

AVOCADO

1923 - 1933

Indiana Glass Company

Dunkirk, Indiana

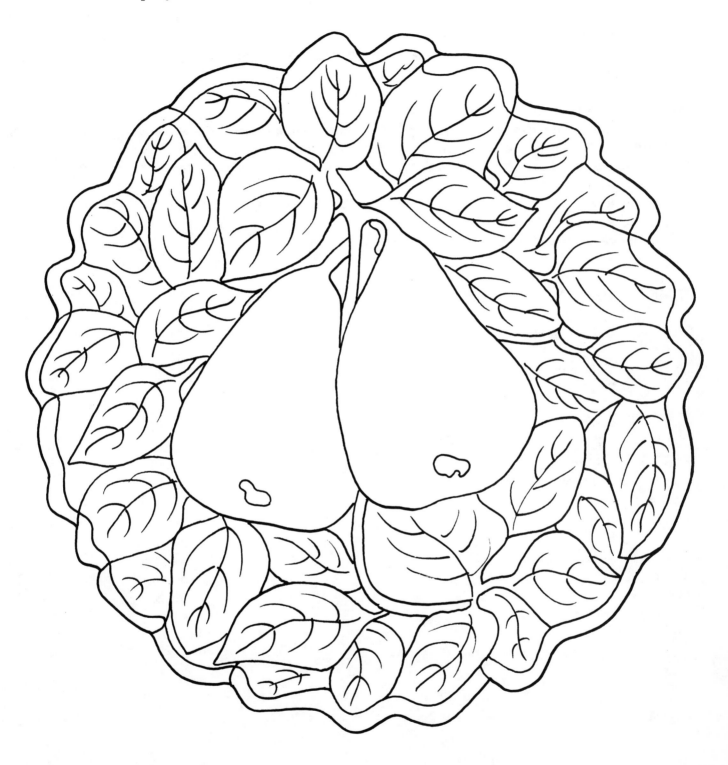

Colors found to date:

- Crystal
- Green
- Pink
- White

Reproductions or Reissues

Back in the early to mid-1970's Indiana Glass introduced what they describe as a reissue (taken from the original molds) of the Avocado pattern in tumblers and a pitcher in pink, red, frosted pink, green, a dark blue or purple color and amber. The only one to worry about presently is the pink. That is the only duplication of the original colors in the pattern. The reissued pink appears to have an orange cast to the color so you should be able to easily identify the new pieces if you can compare them to the old pink color. These new pieces are distributed exclusively through a home party plan by a company named Tiara.

General Pattern Notes

The company calls this their "No. 601 Line" and the name Avocado was given it by collectors. Curiously, early company advertisements refer to it as a **pear** and leaf design. The fruits do resemble avocados, however, and that is what collectors call it. Apparently the company has acquiesced to this with the new issues.

The most difficult to find of the items in this pattern are the pitchers and tumblers in green and most of the saucers.

The whole Avocado pattern line is generally hard to find.

ITEM	DESCRIPTION & REMARKS	DOLLAR VALUE RANGES BY COLOR	
		Green	Pink
Bowl	5¼" (2-handled)	31-36	26-30
Bowl	6" (footed)	27-33	21-26
Bowl	7" (1-handled)	24-29	17-21
Bowl	7½"	53-64	34-40
Bowl	8" (2-handled, oval)	26-30	21-26
Bowl	8½"	48-58	40-50
Bowl	9½"	90-100	62-74
Creamer	(footed)	40-49	34-40
Cup	(footed)	36-44	34-42
Pitcher		600-700	360-430
Plate	6¼"	14-17	10-12
Plate	8¼"	21-26	14-17
Plate	10¼" (cake)	42-52	31-36
Saucer		30-36	26-32
Sherbet		65-82	63-75
Sugar	(footed)	41-48	34-40
Tumbler		143-170	100-120

BAROQUE
1936-1950's

Fostoria Glass Company

Moundsville, Virginia

Colors found to date:
- Azure blue
- Crystal
- Topaz (yellow)

Reproductions or Reissues

None known to date

General Pattern Notes

A very simple and elegant pattern consisting of little ornamentation. The pieces most difficult to find are the footed punch bowls and pitchers in all three colors. There is a plethora of bowls to be found.

ITEM	DESCRIPTION & REMARKS	DOLLAR VALUE RANGES BY COLOR		
		Blue	Crystal	Yellow
Ash Tray		16-20	8-10	13-15
Bowl	3-3/4"	38-44	20-23	33-38
Bowl	4" handled (three types)	17-20	9-11	14-16
Bowl	5"	18-22	10-12	14-16
Bowl	6"	25-30	12-14	22-25
Bowl	6" (square)	15-19	9-11	14-16
Bowl	6-1/2" (2 sections(	15-19	10-12	14-16
Bowl	7' three-footed	22-25	12-14	20-23
Bowl	w/cover, 7-1/2"	41-46	22-25	33-38
Bowl	8-1/2"	28-32	14-16	22-25
Bowl	9-1/2", oval	33-38	20-23	28-32
Bowl	10"	39-44	17-20	33-38
Bowl	10", three sections	30-35	20-23	25-30
Bowl	10" x 7-1/2"	—	22-25	—
Bowl	10-1/2", handled	38-44	20-23	33-38
Bowl	11"	25-30	14-16	22-25
Bowl	11", rolled edge	39-44	22-25	33-38
Bowl	12", flared	34-39	23-26	28-32
Candelabra, two branch		38-44	44-50	55-63
Candlelabra three branch		44-50	55-62	36-42
Candlestick (pair) 4"		33-38	18-22	28-32
Candlestick (pair) 4-1/4", two lite		44-50	18-22	38-48
Candlestick (pair) 5-1/2"		38-44	20-23	33-38
Candlestick (pair) 6", three lite		55-62	33-38	44-50
Candlestick (pair) 7-3/4"		44-50	28-32	39-44
Candy	w/cover three section	41-46	23-26	33-38
Celery	11", oval	25-30	14-16	22-25
Compote	4-3/4"	22-25	10-12	18-22
Compote	6-1/2"	24-28	9-11	20-23
Creamer	3-1/4", individual	12-14	7-9	11-13
Sugar	3", individual	12-14	6-8	11-13
Creamer	3-3/4", footed	13-15	8-10	13-15
Sugar	3-1/2", footed	12-14	7-9	12-14
Cruet w/top 5-1/2"		250-280	28-32	220-245
Cup	footed	16-20	7-9	12-14
Punch Cup 6 ounce		16-20	8-10	14-16
Ice Bucket		55-62	24-28	50-58
Mayonnaise with underplate		38-48	17-20	32-37
Pitcher	6-1/2"	550-605	165-185	435-485
Pitcher	7"	520-585	135-152	420-470
Plate	6"	6-8	3-4	4-5
Plate	7"	10-12	4-5	8-10
Plate	8"	12-14	7-9	10-12

ITEM	DESCRIPTION & REMARKS	DOLLAR VALUE RANGES BY COLOR		
		Blue	Crystal	Yellow
Plate	9"	27-31	13-15	25-30
Plate	10"	23-26	11-13	22-25
Plate	11", center handled	—	16-20	—
Plate	14"	30-35	14-16	25-30
Platter	12", oval	35-40	17-20	33-38
Punch Bowl, footed, one gallon plus		550-605	165-285	440-490
Salt/Pepper Pair		92-105	28-32	82-95
Salt/Peppers Individual (pair)		—	38-48	—
Saucers		6-8	2-3	4-5
Sherbet	3-3/4"	20-23	9-11	17-20
Tray	11", oval	24-28	11-13	20-23
Tray	6-3/4", two-handled	11-13	7-8	9-11
Tumbler	3", footed	18-22	10-12	15-18
Tumbler	3-1/2", 6-1/2 oz.	22-25	11-13	20-23
Tumbler	3-3/4"	24-28	9-11	20-23
Tumbler	5-3/4"	33-38	17-20	27-32
Vase	7"	44-50	17-20	41-46

BEADED BLOCK

c. 1930

Imperial Glass Company

Bellaire, Ohio

Drawing above is of a cross-section showing the high relief of this pattern.

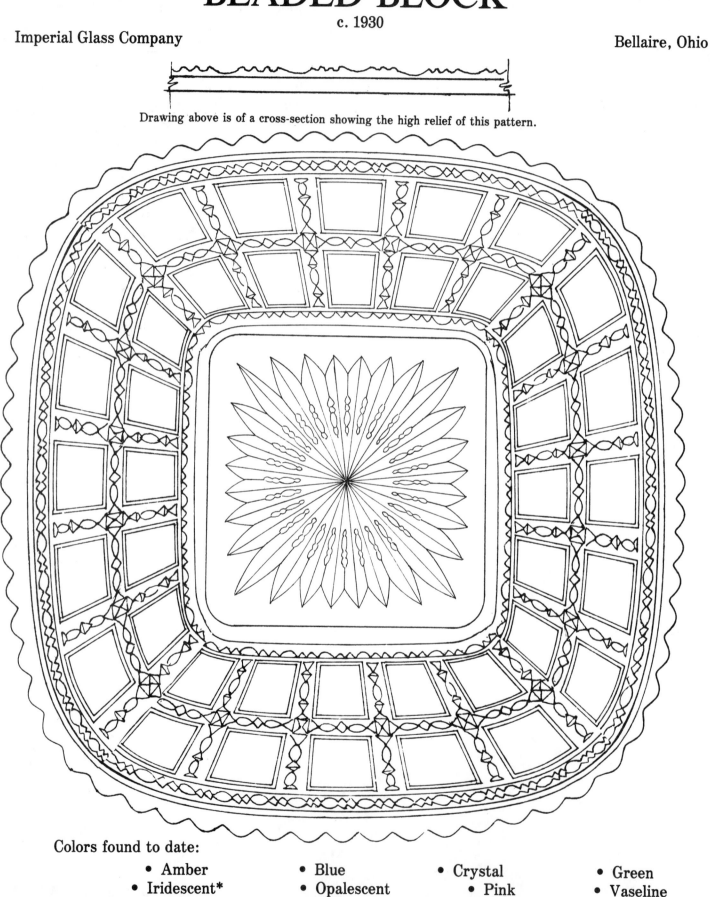

Colors found to date:

- Amber
- Iridescent*
- Blue
- Opalescent
- Crystal
- Pink
- Green
- Vaseline

* Still being manufactured in pink.

Reproductions or reissues
   None found to date

General Pattern Notes

This pattern has a good heavy, quality feel to it. You would almost believe it to be a much higher quality glass than that which is normally associated with depression glass. As the footnote indicates some items are still being produced today. One easy way to identify the newer pieces is to look for a small "IG" mold embossed on the plate. The company began adding this trademark in February of 1951.

ITEM	DESCRIPTION & REMARKS	DOLLAR VALUE RANGES BY COLOR				
		Amber	Crystal	Green	Pink *	Other Colors
Bowl	4½" (2-handled)	8-10	8-10	8-10	8-10	16-20
Bowl	4½" (round lily)	11-14	11-14	11-14	11-14	20-25
Bowl	5½" (square)	7-10	7-10	7-10	7-10	10-12
Bowl	5½" (1 handle)	9-12	9-12	9-12	9-12	11-14
Bowl	6" (round)	11-13	11-13	11-13	11-13	18-20
Bowl	6¼" (round)	9-12	9-12	9-12	9-12	18-20
Bowl	6½" (round)	9-12	9-12	9-12	9-12	18-20
Bowl	6½" (2-handled)	14-15	14-15	14-15	14-15	20-24
Bowl	6¾" (round)	11-14	11-14	11-14	11-14	18-20
Bowl	7¼" (round)	10-12	10-12	10-12	10-12	20-28
Bowl	7½" (round, fluted edge)	23-28	23-28	23-28	23-28	—
Bowl	7½" (round)	10-12	10-12	10-12	10-12	18-20
Bowl	8¼" (celery)	11-14	11-14	11-14	11-14	19-21
Creamer		11-14	11-14	11-14	11-14	21-26
Pitcher	5¼"	155-187	155-187	155-187	155-187	—
Plate	7¾" (square)	7-8	7-8	7-8	7-8	10-12
Plate	8¾"	8-9	8-9	8-9	8-9	14-16
Stemmed Jelly	4½"	9-12	9-12	9-12	9-12	18-20
Stemmed Jelly	4½" (flared lid)	11-14	11-14	11-14	11-14	21-26
Sugar		12-16	12-16	12-16	12-16	21-26
Vase	6"	10-12	10-12	10-12	10-12	21-26

*Still being manufactured in pink.

BLOCK OPTIC

1929 - 1933

Hocking Glass Company

(now Anchor-Hocking Glass Corporation)

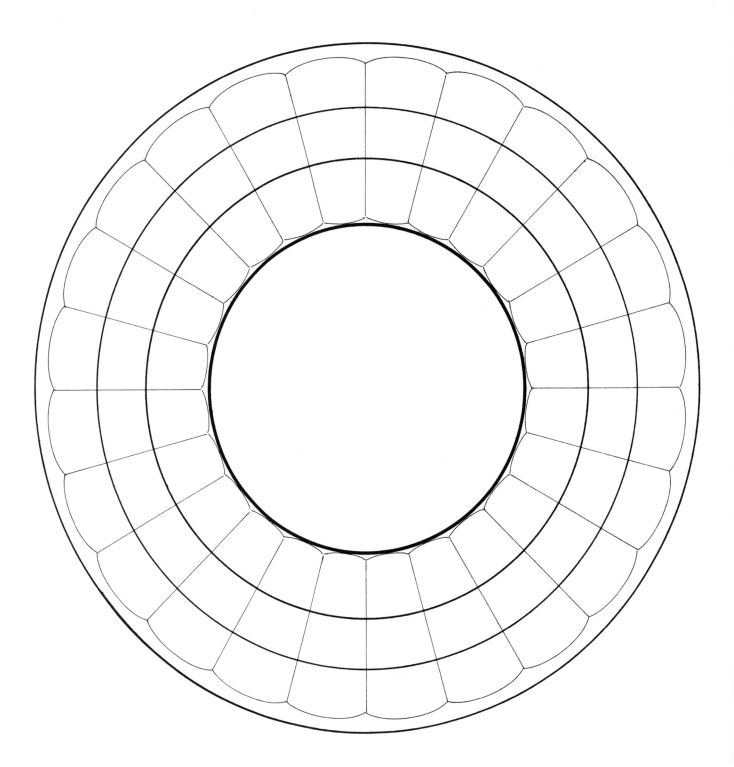

Colors found to date:

• Crystal • Green • Pink • Yellow

BLOCK OPTIC

Reproductions or Reissues
None found to date.

General Pattern Notes
Sometimes known simply as "Block", Block Optic is heard more often today.

Green was the color produced most and yellow is difficult to uncover in any quantity. There were a small number of pieces produced in a satin or frosty finish. It may be that only the sugar and creamer was made with the satin finish, but keep your eyes open. The items with black stems and/or bases are quite elusive. Other scarce pieces are the odd items such as candlesticks, vases, mugs, etc.

You might also note that there is no round butter dish to be found in Block Optic. All that have ever turned up are rectangular. The dinner plate has a snowflake design in the center.

ITEM	DESCRIPTION & REMARKS	DOLLAR VALUE RANGES BY COLOR		
		Green	Pink	Yellow
Bowl	4¼"	6-8	6-8	—
Bowl	5¼"	10-11	8-10	11-14
Bowl	7"	13-15	11-14	15-19
Bowl	8½"	13-17	13-15	23-27
Butter Dish and cover		40-45	—	—
Candlesticks 1¾"		85-105	60-67	—
Candy Jar and cover		31-38	36-43	55-65
Compote	4"	25-30	50-60	—
Creamers	(5 styles)	11-14	11-14	13-15
Cups	(4 styles)	6-8	4-7	8-10
Goblet	4"	25-30	30-35	—
Goblet	4½"	25-30	30-35	—
Goblet	5¾"	16-22	14-17	—
Goblet	7¼"	26-32	18-22	23-28
Ice Bucket		39-44	33-39	—
Ice or Butter Tub		35-40	75-80	—
Mug		36-44	—	—
Pitcher	7 5/8"	65-70	60-65	—
Pitcher	8"	48-52	55-60	—
Pitcher	8½"	36-44	36-44	—
Plate	6"	3-7	3-7	3-7
Plate	8¼"	3-7	3-7	3-7
Plate	9"	15-19	23-27	20-23
Plate	9" (grill)	10-12	13-19	—
Plate	10¼"	18-22	18-22	—
Salt and Pepper (footed) pr.		30-35	60-70	82-93
Salt and Pepper		60-65	—	—
Sandwich Server (center-handled)		46-52	46-52	—
Saucer	5¾"	6-9	6-9	—
Saucer	6 1/8"	6-9	6-9	11-14
Sherbet	(cone shape)	6-8	—	—

BLOCK OPTIC

ITEM	DESCRIPTION & REMARKS	DOLLAR VALUE RANGES BY COLOR		
Sherbet	3¼"	7-9	7-9	11-14
Sherbet	4¾"	13-15	11-14	15-19
Sugar	(3 styles)	11-14	11-14	13-15
Tumbler	3½"	14-19	14-19	—
Tumbler	4" (footed)	13-18	16-22	—
Tumbler	9 oz.	11-14	11-14	—
Tumbler	9 oz. (footed)	14-18	13-16	19-23
Tumbler	10 oz.	14-18	13-15	—
Tumbler	6", 10 oz. (footed)	19-24	19-25	23-27
"Tumble-up Night Set" (3" tumbler and bottle)		60-70	—	—
Vase	5¾"	180-230	—	—
Whiskey Jigger	2½"	20-23	16-22	—

Key For Cover Photos

GREEN	TOPAZ or YELLOW	ULTRAMARINE	AMBER (Light)
CREMAX	FOREST GREEN	PINK	FROSTED or PINK SATIN FINISH
PINK (Orange Cast)	MONAX	**COBALT**	GREEN OPALESCENT

FRONT COVER

BACK COVER

CRYSTAL	RUBY RED	CRYSTAL on METAL BASE	IRIDESCENT
JADITE	LIGHT BLUE	DELPHITE	AMETHYST
SHELL PINK	AMBER (Dark)	OPALESCENT	IRIDESCENT

BOWKNOT

c. 1930
Manufacturer Unknown

Colors found to date:

- Crystal (rare)

- Green

BOWKNOT

Reproductions or Reissues
None found to date.

General Pattern Notes
Little can be said about this pattern named Bowknot by collectors until some evidence surfaces as to manufacturer. It appears always in green but there has been an unsubstantiated report of its being found in crystal.

The listing of eight pieces below includes a saucer because of the known cups. As yet no saucers have turned up.

ITEM	DESCRIPTION & REMARKS	DOLLAR VALUE RANGES BY COLOR
		Green
Bowl	4½"	10-12
Bowl	5½"	13-15
Cup		9-12
Saucer		—
Plate	7"	8-10
Sherbet	(footed)	10-12
Tumbler	5"	11-14
Tumbler	5" (footed)	11-15

BUBBLE

(see General Pattern Notes for dates)

Hocking Glass Corporation

(now Anchor Hocking Glass Corporation)

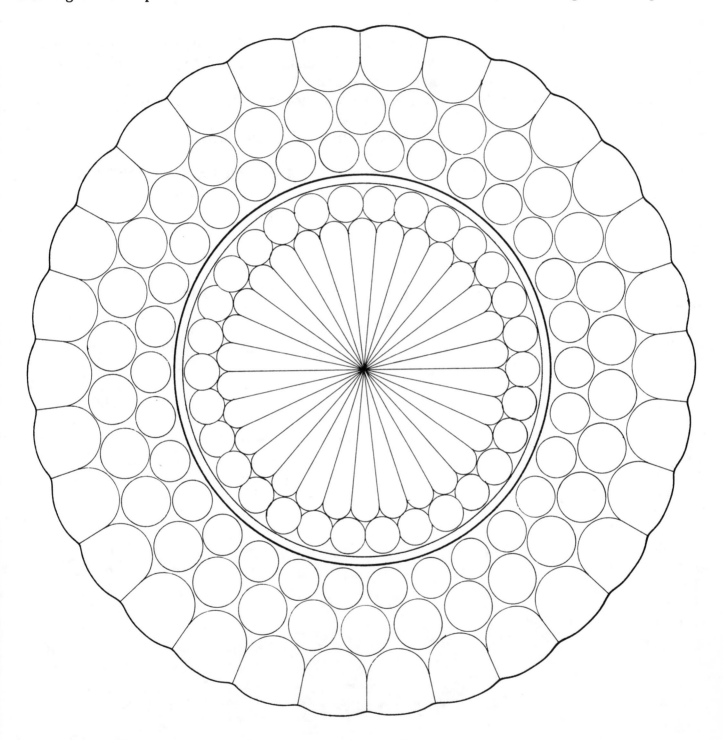

Colors to be found:

- Blue (pale)
- Pink
- Crystal
- Ruby Red
- Green (dark)
- White (milk white)

BUBBLE

Reproductions or Reissues
None found to date.

General Pattern Notes
Bubble has been variously known as "Bullseye" and "Provincial" in the past due to the company issuing the pattern under those names as well. The names referred to new color issues in the pattern and make it fairly easy to date most of the items.

The green ("Forest Green") and the crystal were issued in 1937; the Ruby Red was issued late, in 1963; the pale or light blue was first issued in 1937.

Some of the more rare pieces are the creamer in blue and any flanged bowl.

ITEM	DESCRIPTION & REMARKS	DOLLAR VALUE RANGES BY COLOR			
		Blue	Green	Red	Crystal
Bowl	4"	11-13	3-6	—	2-6
Bowl	4½"	7-9	3-6	4-7	2-6
Bowl	5¼"	7-9	3-6	—	3-8
Bowl	7¾"	12-16	—	—	8-13
Bowl	8 3/8"	12-16	11-12	—	8-13
Bowl	9" (flanged)	54-64	—	—	—
Candlesticks		—	25-30	—	15-21
Creamer		30-35	7-9	—	8-13
Cup		4-6	3-6	7-9	2-6
Lamp		—	—	—	31-40
Pitcher		—	—	54-64	38-47
Plate	6¾"	3-6	2-5	—	2-5
Plate	9 3/8" (grill)	15-20	—	—	—
Plate	9 3/8"	12-18	6-9	10-12	6-9
Platter	12" (oval)	15-20	—	—	12-15
Saucer		2-6	1-4	2-6	1-4
Sugar		15-20	6-9	—	8-13
Tid Bit	(2-level)	—	—	25-30	—
Tumbler	6 oz.	—	—	10-12	3-7
Tumbler	9 oz.	—	—	8-11	7-11
Tumbler	12 oz.	—	—	14-17	—
Tumbler	16 oz.	—	—	21-26	—
Tumbler	16 oz. (footed)	—	—	—	15-19

CAMEO

1930 - 1934

Hocking Glass Company   (now Anchor Hocking Glass Corporation)

CAMEO. Note
the dancing girl or ballerina
within the cameo portion of the design. Turn
to the ROSE CAMEO pattern and compare in order to
avoid confusing the two patterns.

Colors found to date:

- Crystal
- Pink
- Crystal (with platinum rim)
- Yellow ("Topaz")
- Green

CAMEO

Reproductions or Reissues

The salt and pepper shakers were reproduced in pink. This writer has not seen them but dealers have spoken of them as having a light or faint pattern when compared to the genuine pieces. They appeared in 1982. There is a modern addition to the pattern. Found in pink, green or gold, they are child-size pieces, tumblers, ice bucket, a footed bowl, plates, cups, saucers, creamers, sugars, butter dishes and candle holders. They are technically not reproductions for they were never produced as a part of the original line.

General Pattern Notes

The Cameo (also known as "Ballerina" and "Dancing Girl") is one of the most popularly collected depression glass patterns. It is also widely available due to the enormous number of pieces manufactured. Some, however, are extremely rare and valuable (note the prices in the listing). The rarest of all is of course the center handle sandwich server, but then so are all the center-ringed or cup-ringed saucers. Unless you own a gold mine, give up the idea of a complete set, but you can still gather a useful set of basic pieces for a reasonable outlay.

ITEM	DESCRIPTION & REMARKS	DOLLAR VALUE RANGES BY COLOR			
		Crystal	Green	Pink	Yellow (Topaz)
Bowl	4¼"	7-9	—	—	
Bowl	4¾" (cream soup)	—	84-94	—	—
Bowl	5½"	6-7	24-29	—	25-30
Bowl	7¼"	—	42-49	—	
Bowl	8¼"	—	42-49	—	63-73
Bowl	9" (rimmed)	—	44-53	—	—
Bowl	10" (oval)	—	18-23	—	32-38
Bowl	11" (console, 3-legged)	—	72-82	32-37	96-106
Butter Dish (covered)		—	180-205	—	840-890
Cake Plate	10" (3-legged)	—	24-29	—	—
Cake Plate	10½"	—	90-100	—	—
Candlesticks	4" (pair)	—	100-109	—	—
Candy Jar	4" (covered)	—	66-79	455-465	90-105
Candy Jar	6½" (covered)	—	150-175	—	—
Cocktail Shaker (metal lid)		240-290	—	—	—
Compote	5"	—	32-38	—	—
Cookie Jar with cover		—	60-70	—	—
Creamer	3¼"	—	30-35	—	21-26
Creamer	4¼"	—	29-33	90-100	—
Cup	(2 styles)	—	18-21	90-100	12-14
Decanter	10" (with stopper)	—	112-126	—	—
Decanter	10" (with stopper, frosted)	—	38-44	—	—
Domino Tray	7" (3" ring)	—	104-115	—	—
Domino Tray	7" (no ring)	155-190	—	216-236	—
Goblet	3½"	—	180-205	—	—
Goblet	4"	—	78-88	245-270	—
Goblet	6"	—	54-64	190-230	—
Ice Bowl	(3" x 5½")	240-290	150-180	495-570	
Jar	2" (covered)	165-200	132-152	—	—
*Pitcher	5¾"	—	190-216	—	285-335
*Pitcher	6"	—	62-75	—	—
*Pitcher	8½"	325-365	62-70	—	—

* Some pitchers have a rope design ringing the pitcher just below the top.

ITEM	DESCRIPTION & REMARKS	Crystal	Green	Pink	Yellow (Topaz)
			DOLLAR VALUE RANGES BY COLOR		
Plate	6"	3-7	3-7	52-75	3-6
Plate	7"	3-7	—	—	—
Plate	8"	4-8	12-14	42-49	3-7
Plate	8½" (square)	—	36-41	—	105-117
Plate	9½"	—	19-22	54-63	12-14
Plate	10"	—	14-17	54-63	—
Plate	10½" (grill)	—	13-17	62-74	12-14
Plate	10½" (grill, closed handles)	—	48-58	—	9-12
Plate	11½" (closed handles)	—	12-14	—	8-12
Platter	12" (closed handles)	—	24-28	—	24-30
Relish	7½" (footed, 3 sections)	—	24-28	—	90-100
Salt and Pepper (pair, footed)		—	78-90	575-650*	—
Sandwich Server (center handled)		—	1400-1600	—	—
Saucer	(cup ringed)	—	90-100	—	—
Saucer	6" (same as sherbet, plate)	—	3-7	62-75	3-6
Sherbet	3 1/8"	—	15-20	46-53	27-32
Sherbet	4 7/8"	—	36-41	90-100	42-48
Sugar	3¼"	—	15-21	—	15-21
Sugar	4¼"	—	24-30	76-87	—
Tumbler	3¾"	—	30-37	105-117	—
Tumbler	4"	13-17	24-31	105-117	—
Tumbler	4¾"	—	31-35	—	—
Tumbler	5"	—	31-35	126-146	42-48
Tumbler	5¼"	—	44-54	—	—
Tumbler	3 oz. (footed)	—	62-75	139-157	—
Tumbler	5", 9 oz. (footed)	—	29-33	132-152	20-24
Tumbler	5¾" (footed)	—	42-51	—	—
Tumbler	6 3/8"	—	180-230	—	—
Vase	5¾"	—	150-175	—	—
Vase	8"	—	31-37	—	—
Water Bottle	(Whitehouse vinegar)	—	31-37	—	—

*Still being manufactured in pink, this value is for the older, original pair.

CHERRYBERRY

c. 1930

(See STRAWBERRY, page 172)

CHERRY BLOSSOM

1930's

Jeannette Glass Company   Jeannette, Pennsylvania

Colors found to date:

- Crystal (odd pieces)
  - Jadite (opaque green)
- Delphite (opaque blue)
  - Pink
- Green
- Red

CHERRY BLOSSOM

Reproductions or Reissues

Many pieces of Cherry Blossom have been reproduced and available from the A.A. Importing Co., Inc. The following is a listing of those pieces that are on the market, all in pink, green or red.

Butter Dish (covered)
Pitcher (6¾"
Tumblers (4 3/8", footed)
Salad Plate (6")
Bowl (6")
Bowl (8 3/8")
Salt and Pepper Shakers (Delphite. This color never made in original line salt & peppers)
Tray (12")

Dinner Plate (9")
Cup and Saucer
Butter Dish (red)
Pitcher (red)
Tumbler (red)

The major identifying differences between the old and new follows:

Pitchers — old have nine cherries on the underside of the base. The new ones only have seven.

Tumblers — old have either two or three separate, close rings around the edge just below the lip. The new tumblers have only one single ring there.

Shakers* — The easiest way to tell new from old is the amount of solid glass in the bottom inside down at the base. The new ones have more than twice as much solid glass than the old.

Butter Dishes — The flange pattern on the old ones extends right out to the edge of the rim and on the new ones, the pattern stops short of the rim.

The overall pattern quality on all these pieces is definitely lower than the originals.

Another reproduction of unknown source is that of the child's set. The original set was called "Jeannette's Junior Dinner Set" and consisted of four each of 6" plates, cups and saucers, a creamer and an uncovered sugar bowl for a total of 14 pieces. They are scaled down to about one-third of the regular tableware size and were available in pink and delphite.

The reproductions are of decidedly lower quality in color, pattern and overall appearance. Some of them even have upside-down designs. The reproductions are of a cup, saucer and, for some unknown reason, a butter dish. The cup and saucer appear in pink and delphite; the butter dish was made in cobalt blue. No problem there for the original butter dish was never made in that color. The cups and saucers are crude copies at best.

General Pattern Notes

Cherry Blossom is also a popular, heavily collected pattern in depression glass.

Some significant variations are due to design changes over the years. For instance, in the first years of production all footed pieces sported round bases. They were later given scalloped bases but not exclusively. The best way to identify a newer one is by its shape. The earlier pitchers were cone-shaped while the newer ones were more rounded.

The delphite color didn't appear until about 1936.

All the salt and pepper shakers are quite rare and hard to find.

The patterns are also known to appear all over an item or on the top only.

Salt and pepper shakers appear in pink and green only.

* A few of the reproduction shakers were dated "77" on the base, but not all.

ITEM	DESCRIPTION & REMARKS	DOLLAR VALUE RANGES BY COLOR			
		Delphite	Green	Jadite	Pink
Bowl	4¾"	13-17	12-15	—	10-13
Bowl	5¾"	—	24-29	—	26-32
Bowl	7¾"	—	46-54	—	40-50
Bowl	8½"	54-64	20-25	—	17-20
Bowl	9" (oval)	56-65	23-27	—	21-25
Bowl	9" (2-handled)	18-21	23-27	265-335	19-23
Bowl	10½" (3-legged)	—	45-58	260-345	45-54
Butter Dish and cover		—	98-118	—	85-98
Cake Tray	10¼" (3-legged)	—	22-27	—	21-25
Coaster		—	12-16	—	14-17
Creamer		22-27	16-20	—	13-16
Cup		19-24	17-22	—	16-20
Mug		—	135-162	—	150-190
Pitcher	6¾"	—	50-60	—	40-50
Pitcher	7"	—	44-52	—	35-45
Pitcher	8" (footed)	110-130	58-73	—	40-50
Plate	6"	12-14	7-9	—	5-8
Plate	7"	—	17-22	—	17-20
Plate	9"	15-18	18-23	40-50	14-17
Plate	9" (grill)	—	22-26	—	22-26
Plate	10" (grill)	—	45-58	—	—
Platter	9" (oval)	—	—	—	600-675
Platter	11" (oval)	40-50	27-33	—	25-30
Platter	13" (also 13" sectioned)	—	45-58	—	45-52
Salt and Pepper		—	750-900	—	1000-1200
Saucer		5-7	4-7	—	5-7
Sherbet		13-16	14-17	—	12-16
Sugar and cover		22-27	14-16	—	11-13
Tray	(sandwich, 10½")	18-22	21-25	—	17-20
Tumbler	3¾" (footed)	22-27	20-25	—	15-18
Tumbler	4½", 9 oz. (footed)	23-27	33-40	—	30-37
Tumbler	4½", 8 oz. (footed)	23-27	33-40	—	30-37
Tumbler	3½"	—	16-20	—	16-20
Tumbler	4¼"	—	23-27	—	16-20
Tumbler	5"	—	45-58	—	35-45

JEANNETTE'S JUNIOR DINNER SET (Pink or Delphite)

Creamer	28-35
Cup	24-32
Plate	10-14
Saucer	5-8
Sugar	28-35
Entire 14-piece set	185-235

Original box adds about 15.00 to the price.

CIRCLE

Hocking Glass Company

(now Anchor-Hocking Glass Corporation)

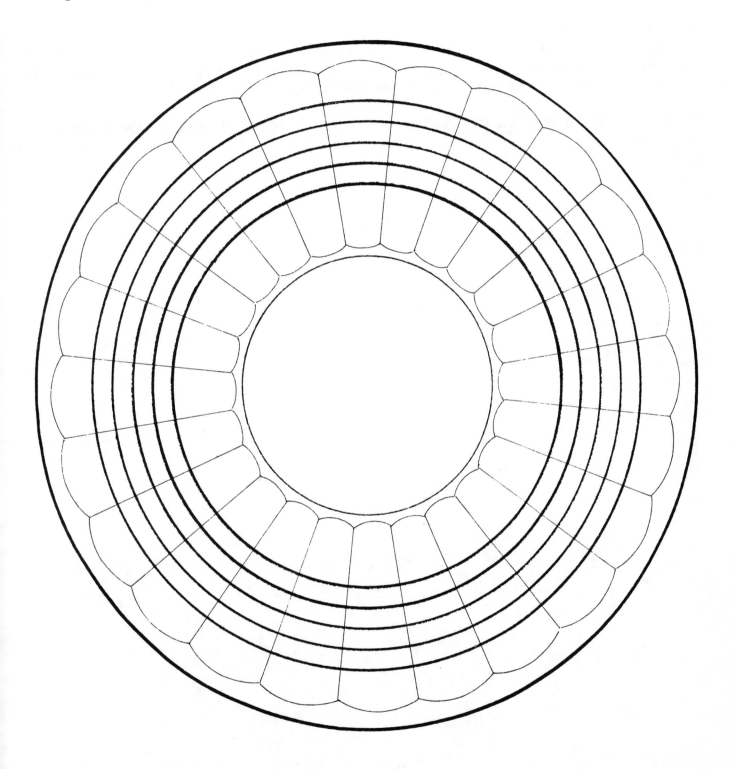

Colors found to date:

- Crystal
- Green
- Pink

Reproductions or Reissues

None known to date.

General Pattern Notes

At present the green color is most commonly found. Some pink is found and so far the crystal exists only as a catalog listing. Some pieces in the pattern have center ray designs but in some they are absent. So far the larger pieces seem to be the hardest to find.

ITEM	DESCRIPTION & REMARKS	DOLLAR VALUE RANGES BY COLOR
		Green or Pink
Bowl	4½"	3-5
Bowl	8"	6-9
Creamer		5-7
Cup	(2 styles)	3-5
Decanter	(with handle)	22-27
Goblet	4½"	4-7
Goblet	8 oz.	7-9
Pitcher		22-27
Plate	6"	3-5
Plate	9½"	5-7
Saucer		1-4
Sherbet	3 1/8"	4-7
Sherbet	4¾"	5-8
Sugar		5-7
Tumbler	4 oz.	4-7
Tumbler	8 oz.	5-7
Vase		21-25

CLOVERLEAF

1931 - 1936

Hazel Atlas Glass Company

Clarksburg, West Virginia and Zanesville, Ohio

Colors found to date:

- Black
- Pink
- Crystal
- Yellow
- Green

CLOVER LEAF

Reproductions or Reissues

None known to date.

General Pattern Notes

Cloverleaf is tough to find in any quantity most of the time with the black being the most elusive of all the colors. It was a small line with only 19 different items offered, based upon what has been uncovered so far. Only ten of these have been found in black.

ITEM	DESCRIPTION & REMARKS	DOLLAR VALUE RANGES BY COLOR			
		Black	Green	Pink	Yellow
Ash Tray	4"	102-112	—	—	—
Ash Tray	5¾"	99-119	—	—	—
Bowl	4"	—	19-23	13-18	23-27
Bowl	5"	—	19-25	—	33-39
Bowl	7"	—	28-35	—	50-60
Bowl	8"	—	49-63	—	—
Candy Dish and cover		—	51-60	—	137-162
Creamer	(footed)	13-17	10-12	—	20-23
Cup		11-15	7-10	7-10	16-22
Plate	6"	26-32	4-8	—	5-9
Plate	8"	15-18	7-10	7-10	14-17
Plate	10¼" (grill)	—	23-27	—	26-32
Salt and Pepper (shaker, pair)		82-93	33-39	—	121-146
Saucer		3-7	3-7	2-6	3-7
Sherbet	(footed)	15-17	5-8	5-9	11-14
Sugar	3 5/8" (footed)	13-17	10-11	—	13-20
Tumbler	4",	—	33-39	—	—
Tumbler	3¾" (flared base)	—	28-35	—	—
Tumbler	5¾" (footed)	—	23-27	33-39	—

COLONIAL

1934 - 1938

Hocking Glass Company   (now Anchor-Hocking Glass Corporation)

Colors found to date:

- Crystal   • Green   • Pink

COLONIAL

Reproductions or Reissues

None known to date.

General Pattern Notes

Colonial is a pattern taken from an elegant, classic old pressed glass design known as "Knife and Fork", hence the commonly used alternate name for the pattern.

The pattern is relatively hard to collect as there aren't too many pieces available today.

An unusual item to be found in depression glass patterns is the "spooner" (spoon or celery holder) but it is found in this pattern.

There seems to be an unusually large number of tumbler styles to choose from though none but the smallest sizes are in anything close to plentiful supply. Mugs are quite rare in any of the colors but a green one would be an exceedingly fine prize.

ITEM	DESCRIPTION & REMARKS	DOLLAR VALUE RANGES BY COLOR		
		Crystal	Green	Pink
Bowl	3¾"	—	—	42-49
Bowl	4½"	4-6	12-15	12-14
Bowl	5½"	13-16	62-70	42-49
Bowl	4½" (cream soup)	—	51-62	44-54
Bowl	7"	14-17	53-63	42-49
Bowl	9"	13-16	24-29	18-21
Bowl	10" (oval)	15-19	30-35	19-24
Butter Dish and cover		51-61	72-82	570-640
Cheese Dish		—	134-154	—
Creamer	5"	12-14	25-29	19-24
Cup		8-10	15-18	7-11
Cordial	3¾"	19-22	36-42	—
Goblet	4"	—	30-36	26-33
Goblet	4½"	—	32-37	26-32
Goblet	5¼"	—	27-32	24-29
Goblet	5¾"	19-23	32-37	30-35
Mug	4½"	—	325-365	185-210
Pitcher	7"	32-37	62-70	50-58
Pitcher	7¾"	36-42	72-87	55-65
Pitcher	(pink with beaded top)	—	—	550-575
Plate	6"	1-5	5-7	3-6
Plate	8½"	4-6	8-12	6-10
Plate	10"	17-21	60-70	32-37
Plate	10" (grill)	12-14	32-37	24-29
Platter	12" (oval)	12-15	24-28	18-21
Salt and Pepper (shaker, pair)		72-84	144-174	140-175
Saucer		1-5	5-7	3-6
Sherbet	3"	—	—	12-15
Sherbet	3 3/8"	5-7	15-18	9-12
Spoon or celery holder (2-handled)		62-70	134-154	130-144
Sugar and cover 6"		20-24	36-42	42-50
Tumbler	3"	7-11	21-26	15-18

COLONIAL

ITEM	DESCRIPTION & REMARKS	DOLLAR VALUE RANGES BY COLOR		
		Crystal	Green	Pink
Tumbler	4"	12-14	25-30	13-16
Tumbler	10 oz.	13-15	30-35	20-25
Tumbler	12 oz.	14-17	42-50	32-41
Tumbler	15 oz.	18-21	102-112	42-49
Tumbler	3¼" (footed)	12-14	24-28	15-19
Tumbler	4", 5 oz. (footed)	13-15	42-49	24-28
Tumbler	5¼" (footed)	14-17	30-35	24-29
Whiskey Jigger	2½"	5-8	15-18	12-15

Key For Cover Photos

GREEN	TOPAZ or YELLOW	ULTRAMARINE	AMBER (Light)
CREMAX	FOREST GREEN	PINK	FROSTED or PINK SATIN FINISH
PINK (Orange Cast)	MONAX	COBALT	GREEN OPALESCENT

FRONT COVER

BACK COVER

CRYSTAL	RUBY RED	CRYSTAL on METAL BASE	IRIDESCENT
JADITE	LIGHT BLUE	DELPHITE	AMETHYST
SHELL PINK	AMBER (Dark)	OPALESCENT	IRIDESCENT

COLONIAL BLOCK

1930's

Hazel Atlas Glass Company   Clarksburg, West Virginia and Zanesville, Ohio

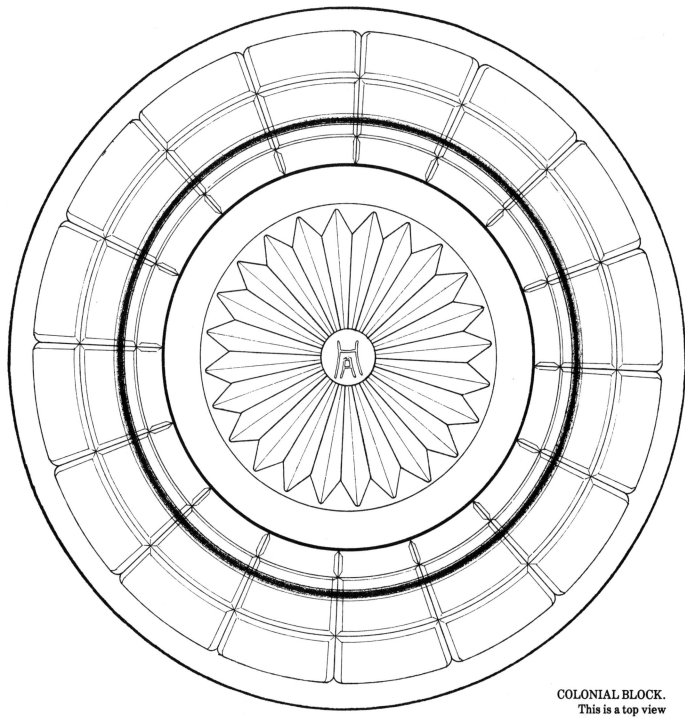

COLONIAL BLOCK.
This is a top view
drawing of the butter dish with cover or lid
removed. Note the Hazel Atlas Glass Company trademark in the center.

Colors found to date:

• Green   • Pink   • White*

*1950's production only. Value ranges from $4.00 to $7.50.

44

COLONIAL BLOCK

Reproductions or Reissues
None known to date.

General Pattern Notes
This is a relatively minor pattern of depression glass. Its inclusion is because of its similarity to the Block Optic pattern and the butter dish frequently being mistaken for Block Optic.

ITEM	DESCRIPTION & REMARKS	DOLLAR VALUE RANGES BY COLOR
		Green or Pink
Bowl	4"	5 - 6
Bowl	7"	12 - 15
Butter Dish		30 - 37
Candy Jar (covered)		28 - 34
Creamer		8 - 12
Sugar and cover		14 - 18

COLONIAL FLUTED

c. 1930

Federal Glass Company

Columbus, Ohio

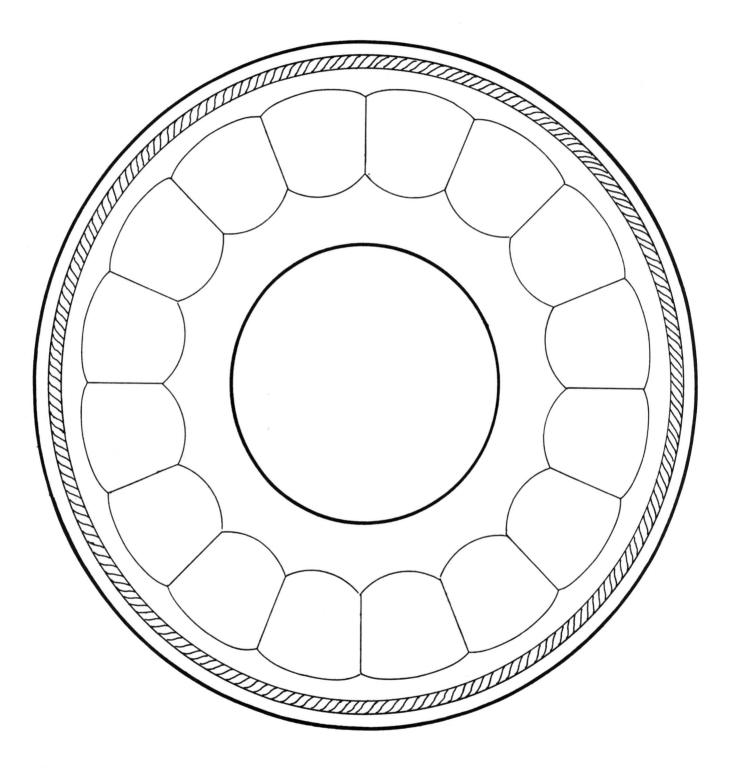

Colors found to date:

- Crystal
- Green
- Pink

COLONIAL FLUTED

Reproductions or Reissues
    None known to date.

General Pattern Notes
    Federal has made it easy to spot their products by frequently, but not always, using their trademark. It is easily recognizable when it appears; an "F" within a shield.
    The pattern is also known as "Rope" because of the rope-like border design.
    There has been no dinner plate size found so far that can be truly labelled Colonial Fluted. There is another Federal Glass Company design that is quite similar, but it lacks the rope border design described above. Whether it is or is not Colonial Fluted has to be a matter of the collector's personal opinion until further evidence is found.
    A particularly attractive variation in the pattern is "The Bridgette Set". These are 6 pieces that can be found with hearts, diamonds, clubs and spades fired on the plates in red and black enamel.

ITEM	DESCRIPTION & REMARKS	DOLLAR VALUE RANGES BY COLOR
		Green
Bowl	4"	4-7
Bowl	6"	5-8
Bowl	6½"	11-13
Bowl	7½"	12-15
Creamer		5-7
Cup		3-5
Plate	6"	2-4
Plate	8"	3-5
Saucer		2-4
Sherbet		5-7
Sugar and cover		12-17

COLUMBIA

1938 - early 1940's

Federal Glass Company

Columbus, Ohio

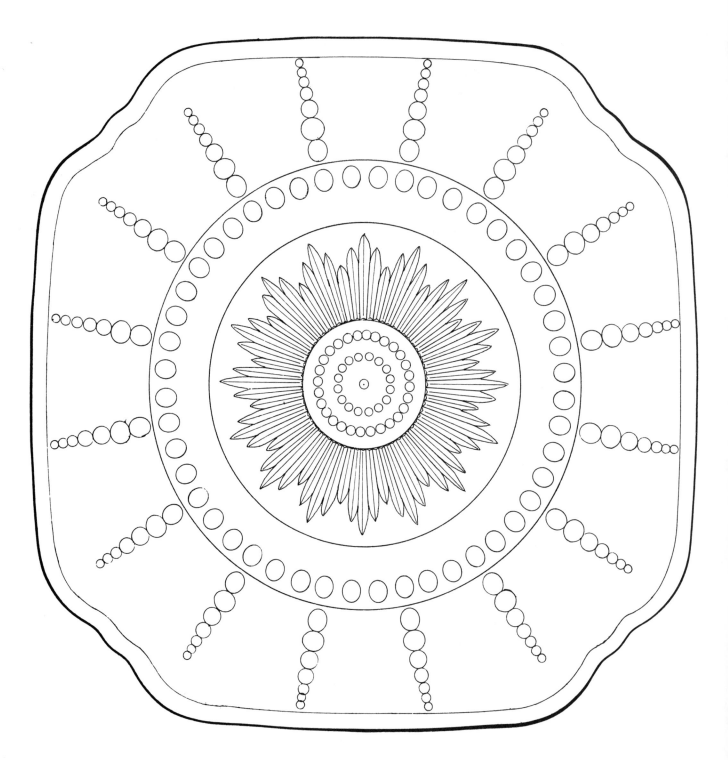

Colors found to date:

- Crystal
- Green
- Pink

COLUMBIA

Reproductions or Reissues
    None known to date.

General Pattern Notes
    First issued in pink in 1938 it quickly was changed to crystal. There are therefore few pink pieces to be found. Indeed, only four pieces were made in pink (see listing). Others in this pattern may be found with gold rims and various color decorations on butter dish covers.

| ITEM | DESCRIPTION & REMARKS | DOLLAR VALUE RANGES BY COLOR | |
		Crystal	Pink
Bowl	5"	7-9	—
Bowl	8"	9-11	—
Bowl	8½"	9-11	—
Bowl	10½" (ruffled edge)	13-17	—
Butter Dish and cover		22-28	—
Cup		3-6	10-12
Plate	6"	2-3	5-7
Plate	9½"	4-6	13-17
Plate	11¾"	8-9	—
Saucer		1-2	5-9
Snack Plate		30-35	—
Tumbler 4 oz.		15-20	—
Tumbler 9 oz.		20-25	—

CORONATION

1936 - 1940

Hocking Glass Company

(now Anchor-Hocking Glass Corporation)

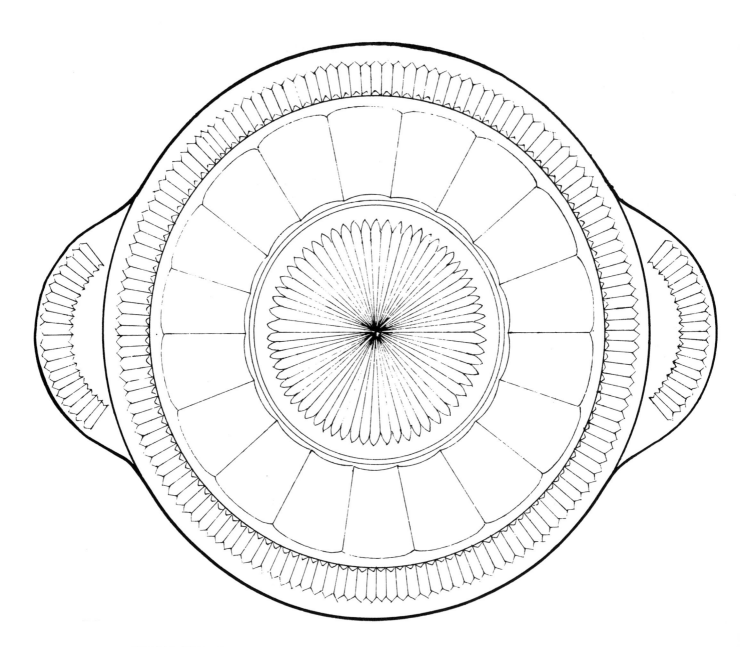

CORONATION. Drawing shows top view of a 4½" berry bowl with closed handles (no holes in the handles). The same bowl can be found with open handles. The bowl pattern design remains the same but the pattern design in the handles differs slightly from that of the closed handle bowls.

Colors found to date:

- Crystal
- Pink
- Ruby Red

CORONATION

Reproductions or Reissues
None known to date.

General Pattern Notes
Be very careful not to confuse the tumblers in this pattern with "Lace Edge" pattern tumblers. This frequently causes much inconvenience in buying or trading among dealers and collectors alike. The ray designs in the Coronation pattern tumblers ascend much farther up the side than do those on the Lace Edge tumblers.

The handles on ruby red bowls are almost always open.

ITEM	DESCRIPTION & REMARKS	DOLLAR VALUE RANGES BY COLOR	
		Pink	Red
Bowl	4¼"	5-7	6-9
Bowl	6½"	6-8	10-13
Bowl	8"	11-13	14-19
Cup		5-7	6-8
Pitcher		195-210	—
Plate	6"	2-4	—
Plate	8½"	6-9	8-10
Saucer		2-4	—
Sherbet		5-7	6-8
Tumbler	5" (footed)	20-25	—

CUBIST

1929 - 1933

Jeannette Glass Company

Jeannette, Pennsylvania

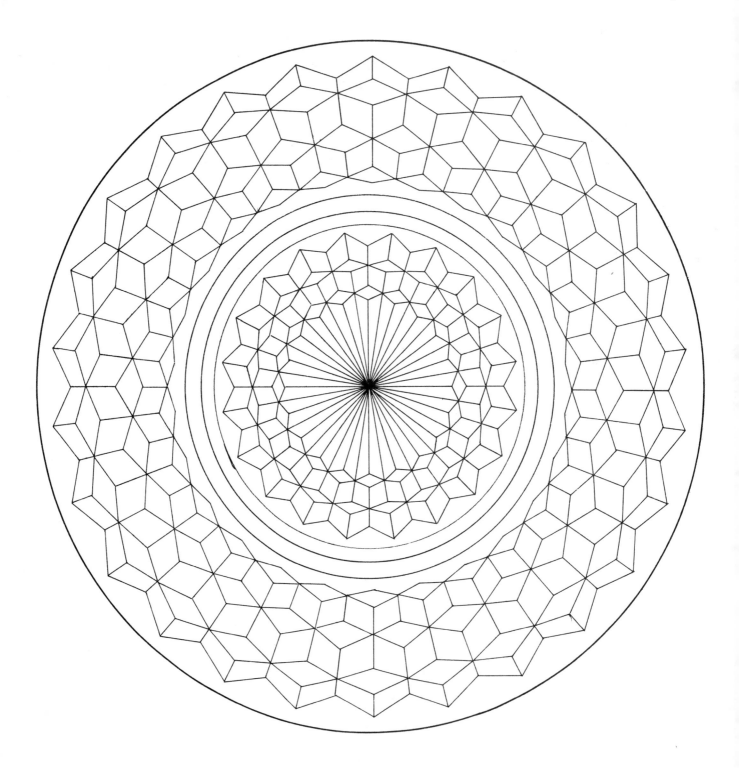

Colors found to date:

- Crystal
- Green
- Pink

CUBIST

Reproductions or Reissues
    None found to date.

General Pattern Notes
    The first thing the collector should be aware of is the extreme similarity between this pattern and the very fine **crystal** pattern "American" by Fostoria. Should you have crystal items in your collection that do not match any of those listed below, then it is probably Fostoria. The depression glass pattern of Cubist is nearly the same, but the quality is far below that of the Fostoria crystal.
    The green color wasn't in production long so it isn't easy to find. Crystal was the last color to be added to the line.
    The candy and sugar lids in Cubist are the same and are interchangeable.

ITEM	DESCRIPTION & REMARKS	DOLLAR VALUE RANGES BY COLOR	
		Green	Pink
Bowl	4½"	6-8	4-7
Bowl	4½"	7-10	4-7
Bowl	6½"	16-20	11-12
Butter Dish and cover		69-85	69-85
Candy Jar and cover	6½"	36-43	30-35
Coaster		6-9	4-7
Creamer	2"	—	2-6
Creamer	3"	11-12	6-9
Cup		11-12	4-7
Pitcher	8¾"	150-175	150-175
Plate	6"	3-6	1-4
Plate	8"	6-8	3-6
Powder Jar and cover (3-legged)		25-30	15-21
Salt and Pepper (pair)		37-44	32-39
Saucer		2-4	2-4
Sherbet (footed)		9-11	6-8
Sugar	2"	—	3-6
Sugar	3"	9-11	4-7
Sugar or Candy (covered)		13-16	11-12
Tray for 3" Creamer and Sugar, 7½" (crystal)		—	6-8
Tumbler	4"	42-51	28-32

DAISY

Indiana Glass Company

Dunkirk, Indiana

Colors found to date:

- Amber
- Crystal
- Dark Green

DAISY

Reproductions or Reissues
None known to date.

General Pattern Notes
This pattern was called "No. 620" by the company. Daisy is the name given it by collectors.

The green color, and some white pieces even, are there to be found but collectors should know that these colors are of the 1960's and 1970's vintage, therefore not depression glass. The crystal color is but the most popular color; amber was made during the 1940's.

ITEM	DESCRIPTION & REMARKS	DOLLAR VALUE RANGES BY COLOR	
		Amber	Crystal or Green
Bowl	4½"	10-11	3-6
Bowl	4½" (cream soup)	10-11	4-7
Bowl	6"	24-28	7-10
Bowl	7 3/8"	13-17	5-8
Bowl	9 3/8"	26-33	7-10
Bowl	10" (oval)	16-22	7-10
Creamer	(footed)	9-10	4-8
Cup		5-8	3-6
Plate	6"	2-5	1-3
Plate	7 3/8"	9-10	2-6
Plate	8 3/8"	5-9	2-6
Plate	9 3/8"	7-10	3-7
Plate	10 3/8" (grill)	12-17	4-8
Plate	11½" (sandwich)	13-15	7-10
Platter	10¾"	13-18	7-10
Relish Dish	(3 sections)	20-24	11-13
Saucer		2-4	1-4
Sherbet	(footed)	10-11	4-7
Sugar	(footed)	7-10	4-7
Tumbler	9 oz. (footed)	16-22	7-10
Tumbler	12 oz. (footed)	36-43	13-17

DIAMOND QUILTED

c. 1930

Imperial Glass Company

Bellaire, Ohio

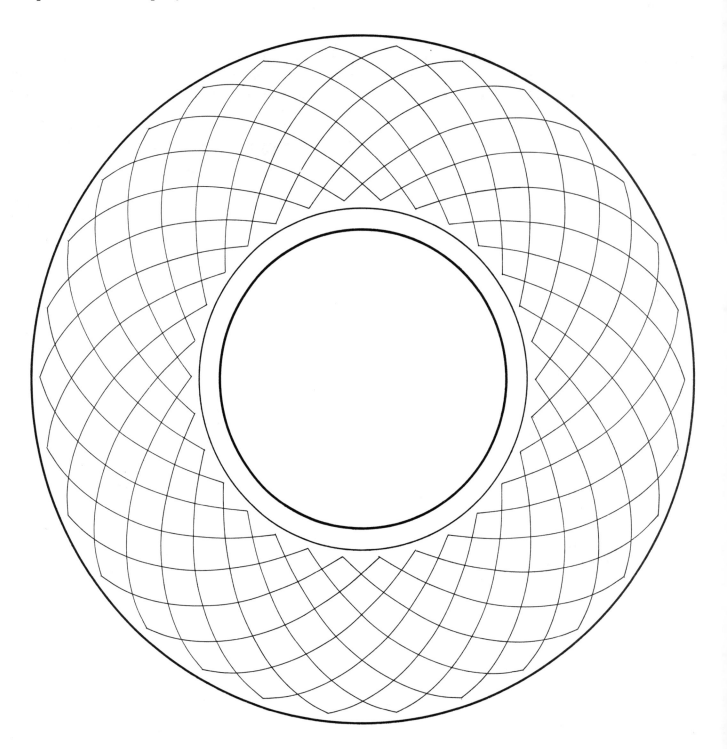

Colors found to date:

- Black
- Blue
- Crystal
- Green
- Pink

Reproductions or Reissues
    None known to date.

General Pattern Notes
    Sometimes known as "Flat Diamond", this pattern was only proven to be a product of Imperial in the recent past.

    The large punch bowl with stand and the champagne bucket are on the top of the scarce list for this pattern.

    Sometimes the pattern appears on the bottom of the black pieces so turn it over when investigating black tableware.

ITEM	DESCRIPTION & REMARKS	DOLLAR VALUE RANGES BY COLOR	
		Black or Blue	Green or Pink
Bowl	4¾" (cream soup)	14-17	10-12
Bowl	5"	10-12	5-8
Bowl	5½" (1-handled)	13-15	7-10
Bowl	7"	13-17	9-10
Bowl	(rolled edge)	33-38	21-25
Bowl	6¼" (covered, footed)	22-24	21-24
Bowl	7¼" (footed)	16-21	15-19
Bowl	7½" (footed)	16-21	15-19
Cake Salver	(10" in diameter)	—	38-47
Candlesticks	(pair)	30-36	13-16
Candy Jar and cover		36-44	23-28
Compote and cover		—	49-62
Creamer		13-16	9-10
Cup		9-10	4-7
Goblet	1 oz.	—	7-10
Goblet	2 oz.	—	7-10
Goblet	3 oz.	—	10-11
Goblet	9 oz. (champagne)	—	11-14
Ice Bucket		82-94	55-65
Mayonnaise Set	(ladle, plate, 3-footed dish)	—	22-28
Pitcher	large	—	33-40
Pitcher	small	—	13-16
Plate	6"	4-7	3-6
Plate	7"	9-10	4-7
Plate	8"	13-17	4-7
Punch Bowl with stand		—	285-315
Plate	14"	14-18	—
Sandwich Server	(center-handled)	32-38	21-25
Saucer		4-7	2-4
Sherbet		11-14	4-7
Sugar		13-15	9-10
Tumbler	9 oz.	—	7-10
Tumbler	12 oz.	—	10-12
Tumbler	6 oz. (footed)	—	7-10
Tumbler	9 oz. (footed)	—	13-15
Tumbler	12 oz. (footed)	—	14-17
Vase	(dolphin handles)	42-52	28-35
Whiskey Jigger	1½ oz.	—	9-10

DIANA

1933 - 1941

Federal Glass Company   Columbus, Ohio

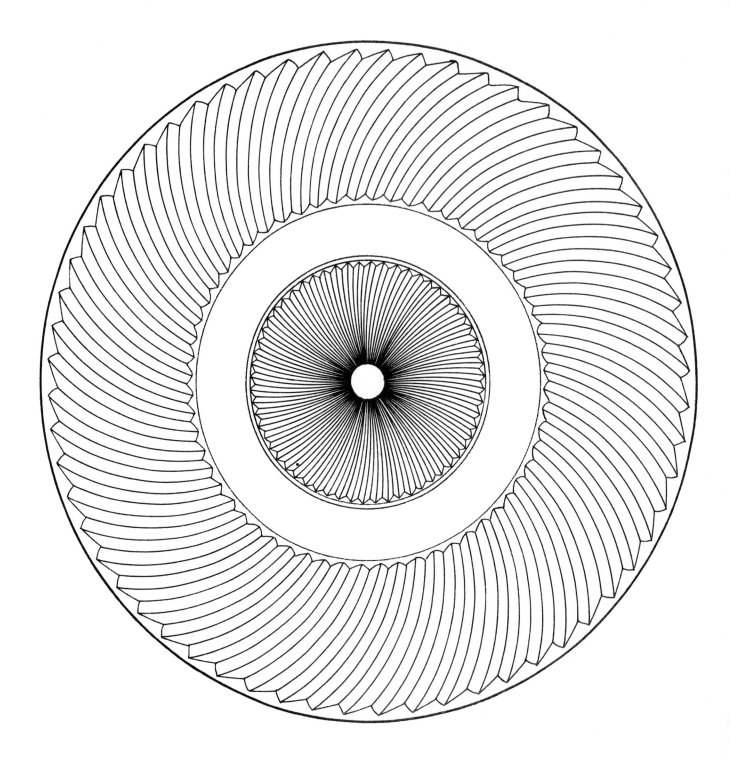

Colors found to date:

- Amber   • Crystal   • Pink

DIANA

Reproductions or Reissues

The 11' console bowl has been reproduced.

General Pattern Notes

First issued in 1933, it was apparently removed from the line sometime later and placed back into production in 1937.

Few odd pieces were made other than the coaster, ash tray, and the small demitasse set.

Some frosted pieces have begun appearing.

ITEM	DESCRIPTION & REMARKS	DOLLAR VALUE RANGES BY COLOR Ambler, Crystal or Pink
Ash Tray	3½"	3-6
Bowl	5"	3-6
Bowl	5½"	7-10
Bowl	9"	10-12
Bowl	11" (console)	10-12
Bowl	12" (scalloped edge)	11-14
Candy Jar	(covered)	26-32
Coaster	3½"	3-6
Creamer		3-7
Cup		4-8
Cup	2 oz. demi-tasse and 4½" saucer (set)	5-9
Plate	5½"	3-7
Plate	6"	1-4
Plate	9½"	5-9
Plate	11¾"	7-10
Platter	12" (oval)	10-12
Salt and Pepper	(pair)	50-85
Saucer		2-4
Sherbet		7-10
Sugar	(no cover)	4-7
Tumbler	4 1/8"	13-15
Junior Set	(6 cups, saucers, plates with upright round rack)	55-67

DOGWOOD

1930 - 1934

Macbeth-Evans Glass Company   Charleroi, Pennsylvania

Colors to be found:

- Cremax   • Crystal*   • Green   • Monax

• Pink   • Yellow*

*Not commonly found. Odd pieces only.

DOGWOOD

Reproductions or Reissues

None known to date.

General Pattern Notes

This pattern is sometimes called "Apple Blossom" or "Wild Rose" by a few collectors, but the pattern is definitely a dogwood motif. The design is usually molded in the typical fashion but there have been some rare occurences of a "silk-screen" acid etched look, usually on pitchers.

Some of the sectioned "grill" style plates have been found with the center design absent. The big twelve-inch oval platter is the most difficult to find as well as the most valuable.

A few of the pieces were quite fragile in that the glass was a bit too thin. So the molds were redesigned to produce a thicker walled piece. Both are still found.

ITEM	DESCRIPTION & REMARKS	DOLLAR VALUE RANGES BY COLOR		
		Green	Monax or Cremax	Pink
Bowl	5½"	26-32	26-32	24-28
Bowl	8½"	70-81	69-86	44-55
Bowl	10¼"	125-170	—	185-235
Cake Plate	11"	—	—	180-245
Cake Plate	13"	86-104	162-197	105-118
Creamer	2½" (thin walled)	57-68	—	14-20
Creamer	3¼" (thick walled)	—	—	24-29
Cup		24-29	62-75	13-18
Pitcher	8", 80 oz.	560-640	—	165-205
Pitcher	8", 80 oz. (American Sweetheart shape)	—	—	620-720
Plate	6"	7-10-	36-44	6-8
Plate	8"	9-12	—	7-8
Plate	9¼"	—	—	26-33
Plate	10½" (grill, either design)	18-23	—	24-29
Plate	12" (salver)	—	33-46	30-37
Platter	12" (oval)	—	—	320-380
Saucer		9-12	30-33	7-8
Sherbet	(footed)	66-81	—	28-35
Sugar	2½" (thin walled)	60-72	—	13-17
Sugar	3¼" (thick walled)	—	—	15-19
Tumbler	3½"	—	—	125-147
Tumbler	4"	84-99	—	36-42
Tumbler	4¾"	100-118	—	40-52
Tumbler	5"	115-127	—	45-60
Tumbler	(etched band)	—	—	14-20
Tid Bit	(8" & 12" plates with metal spindle)	36-44	—	36-46

DORIC and PANSY — DORIC

1937 - 1938   1935 - 1938

Jeannette Glass Company   Jeannette, Pennsylvania

This drawing represents **two** different patterns. The upper half is the "Doric and Pansy",
the lower half is "Doric".

Doric colors found to date:

- Blue (Opaque)   • Crystal   • Delphite   • Green
- Pink   • Topaz   • Yellow

Doric and Pansy colors found to date:

- Crystal   • Pink   • Ultramarine

DORIC

Reproductions or Reissues

None known to date.

General Pattern Notes

Pink, green and delphite are the three colors found most commonly. The others occur rarely and are very difficult to place values upon. If you find any iridescent pieces they are likely of recent vintage.

Occasionally you may find a flower etched on every other panel of the ten-inch sandwich tray.

ITEM	DESCRIPTION & REMARKS	DOLLAR VALUE RANGES BY COLOR		
		Delphite	Green	Pink
Bowl	4½"	42-52	9-12	7-9
Bowl	5" (cream soup)	—	192-232	—
Bowl	5½"	—	33-39	30-35
Bowl	8¼"	132-147	18-21	17-21
Bowl	9" (2-handled)	—	17-21	17-21
Bowl	9" (oval)	—	18-23	17-21
Butter Dish	(covered)	—	112-132	102-119
Cake Plate	10" (3 legs)	—	20-25	21-26
Candy Dish and cover	8"	—	42-49	42-49
Candy Dish	(3 sections)	7-9	8-11	7-10
Coaster	3"	—	18-21	16-21
Creamer	4"	—	14-18	12-15
Cup		—	12-14	8-11
Pitcher	6"	335-385	42-57	38-47
*Pitcher	7½" (footed)	—	770-825	475-525
Plate	6"	—	5-7	3-6
Plate	7"	—	20-25	24-29
Plate	9"	—	13-17	12-15
Plate	9" (grill)	—	18-21	12-15
Platter	12" (oval)	—	18-23	18-23
Relish Tray	(square)	—	12-16	7-10
Relish Tray	4" x 8"	—	17-21	9-12
Salt and Pepper		—	48-57	42-51
Saucer		—	4-7	4-7
Sherbet	(footed)	8-11	13-17	12-15
Sugar and cover		—	42-49	30-35
Tray	10" (handled, sandwich plate)	—	17-21	12-15
Tray	8" x 8"	—	17-21	13-17
Tumbler	4½", 9 oz.	—	65-78	42-49
Tumbler	4", 11 oz.	—	55-65	36-47
Tumbler	5", 12 oz.	—	80-100	42-54

*Yellow - $600

63

Reproductions or Reissues

None known to date.

General Pattern Notes

Doric and Pansy remains a difficult pattern to collect. All colors are scarce. The ultramarine is usually what you encounter when you find it. As with the pink color in the Jeannette products, so does this ultramarine vary widely in hue so don't let it fool you if the colors don't exactly match.

A highly sought set in Doric and Pansy is the child's set called "Pretty Polly Party Dishes". It is a fourteen piece set.

ITEM	DESCRIPTION & REMARKS	DOLLAR VALUE RANGES BY COLOR	
		Crystal or Pink	Ultramarine
Bowl	4½"	11-13	15-17
Bowl	8"	30-37	93-105
Bowl	9" (handled)	15-19	38-46
Butter Dish and cover		--	800-895
Cup		11-15	20-26
Creamer		93-109	214-269
Plate	6"	11-13	13-16
Plate	7"	--	40-47
Plate	9"	7-11	26-30
Salt and Pepper (pair)		--	480-554
Saucer		3-6	7-9
Sugar	(no cover)	99-114	215-270
Tray	10" (handled)	--	30-36
Tumbler	4½"	--	55-65
"PRETTY POLLY PARTY DISHES"			
Creamer		34-41	44-56
Cup		24-30	38-46
Plate		11-13	13-16
Saucer		5-9	6-9
Sugar		34-41	44-56
Entire 14-Piece Set		230-295	340-424

ENGLISH HOBNAIL

1925 - late 1970's

Westmoreland Glass Company

Graperville, Pennsylvania

ENGLISH HOBNAIL. **Make a close
comparison to the MISS AMERICA pattern and make
careful note of the differences. They are explained in the text accompanying each listing.**

Colors found to date:

- Amber
- Blue
- Cobalt
- Crystal
- Green
- Pink
- Red
- Turquoise

ENGLISH HOBNAIL

Reproductions or Reissues

None known to date; however, the company is still in business and may very well reissue one or more at any time. See General Pattern Notes below.

General Pattern Notes

This could well be one of the most confusing of the patterns to collect, but it is also one of the more beautiful so perhaps worth the study necessary to master the complexities.

The pattern was first released in amber and crystal in 1925. In 1929-30 they introduced a variation of crystal by adding black stems to some footed pieces. They also added blue, green and pink to the line around 1926 or so. It goes on and on. A whole book could be devoted to the identification and dating of all the different colors and pieces added over the years.

Westmoreland consistently produced the crystal tableware from the beginning right into the 1970's when even more colors were added. In the 1960's they added another hue of amber but only the well versed collector and dealer can distinguish between the two.

To alleviate any confusion, the collector might well collect it without regard to vintage but only for its beauty.

Values are only a bit higher than the highest range of average. The value list presented here is not classified as to color and is only a sampling of different items available. They very likely approach several hundred in number when different colors and variations due to design change are taken into account.

Be sure to note the similarity of English Hobnail to Miss America. The principal difference is in the lengths of the rays in the center design. The rays in Miss America are uniform in length. Those in Engish Hobnail are in varying lengths.

Values for turquoise and cobalt colors are 100% to 200% higher than those listed below.

ITEM	DESCRIPTION & REMARKS	DOLLAR VALUE RANGES BY COLOR
		All Colors
Ash Tray	(various shapes)	27-33
Bowls	6" (various styles)	14-18
Bowls	8" (various styles)	24-29
Candlesticks	3½" (pair)	38-49
Candlesticks	8½" (pair)	66-76
Celery Dish	9"	22-27
Demitasse Cup and Saucer		33-40
Goblets	(several sizes)	24-29
Lamp	9¼"	130-162
Pitcher	23 oz.	110-140
Pitcher	60 oz.	163-201
Plate	7¼" (pie)	4-8
Plate	10"	24-28
Salt and Pepper (pair)		85-95
Saucer		4-7
Tumbler	4"	21-25
Tumbler	5"	24-29
Tumbler	7 oz. (footed)	17-22
Tumbler	9 oz. (footed)	21-26
*Tumbler	12 oz. (footed)	26-30
Whiskey Jiggers	1½oz & 3 oz.	24-29

*This tumbler has been found with both round (common) and square footed bases.

FLORAGOLD

1950's

Jeanette Glass Company   Jeanette, Pennsylvania

Colors found to date:

- Iridescent   • Crystal   • Blue   • Pink

FLORAGOLD

Reproductions or Reissues
   None found to date

General Pattern Notes
   Floragold is also known by collectors as Louisa. The most commonly found color is the iridescent Amber. This is the first color made with the others being of a later vintage. Rarest piece is the Vase. It looks like a large footed tumbler with a ruffled or scalloped upper edge.

ITEM	DESCRIPTION & REMARKS	DOLLAR VALUE RANGES BY COLOR
		Iridescent
Bowl	4½", squared	3-7
Bowl	5½", round	24-30
Bowl	5½", ruffled	3-7
Bowl	8½", ruffled	3-7
Bowl	8½", squared	12-18
Bowl	9½", ruffled	7-11
Bowl	9½", straight sided	30-40
Bowl	12", ruffled	7-11
Butter Dish	covered, ¼ lb., oblong	21-28
Butter Dish	covered, round	48-56
Candlestick	(pair) Two-branched	42-52
Candy	6¾", covered	42-52
Candy	5¼", 4-footed	3-7
Candy	Single handled	3-7
Coaster	4"	3-7
Creamer		7-11
Cup		3-7
Pitcher	64 ounces	30-50
Plate	5¾"	6-9
Plate	8½"	21-28
Platter	11¼"	18-25
Plate	13½"	17-23
Plate or Tray, 13½", partitioned		42-52
Salt and Pepper plastic tops		48-58
Saucer	5¼"	6-9
Sherbet	footed	9-14
Sugar	covered	17-23
Tumbler	10"	15-18
Tumbler	11"	16-19
Tumbler	15"	60-70

FLORAL

1930 - 1937

Jeannette Glass Company

Jeannette, Pennsylvania

Colors found to date:

- Crystal
- Jadite
- Delphite
- Pink
- Green

FLORAL

Reproductions or Reissues

There exists a very good reproduction of each of the salt and pepper shakers.

General Pattern Notes

This pattern is also sometimes called "Poinsettia". The colors listed on page 69 are the more typical ones, although some very isolated pieces have been found in yellow, amber and red. These should be considered rare unless or until more are found. They may be isolated instances of experimental production, therefore limited in quantity.

The delphite items were made for a short time, being introduced during 1937, the last year of Floral production.

A couple of unusual sets have surfaced; a set of 3 covered bowls in a tray, called a "dresser set" and another, a six-inch utility tray with a ribbed surface.

Look for the design motif beneath the covers on opaque colored items with covers.

Candy lids and sugar lids are identical.

ITEM	DESCRIPTION & REMARKS	Delphite	Green	Pink
Bowl	4"	36-43	13-15	12-15
Bowl	5½" (cream soup)	—	155-180	—
Bowl	7½"	72-87	15-19	14-17
Bowl	8" (covered)	52-71	35-42	32-37
Bowl	9" (oval)	—	17-20	14-16
Butter Dish and cover		—	112-128	105-115
Canister Set (4-piece in Jadite only: 30-35)		—	—	—
Candlesticks 4" (pair)		—	95-108	66-76
Candy Jar and cover		—	39-53	36-44
Creamer		90-102	13-17	12-15
Coaster		—	12-15	10-13
Compote	9"	—	325-400	325-400
Cup		—	12-14	10-13
Dresser Set		—	1110-1250	—
Ice Tub	3½" (oval)	—	445-510	445-510
Lamp		—	120-150	120-150
Pitcher	5½"	—	560-625	—
Pitcher	8" (footed, cone shaped)	—	36-43	28-35
Pitcher	10¼"	—	205-245	175-220
Plate	6"	—	4-7	4-7
Plate	8"	—	10-12	9-11
Plate	9"	72-85	15-19	13-17
Plate	9" (grill)	—	60-70	—
Platter	10¾" (oval)	120-145	17-19	14-17
Refrigerator Dish and cover 5" x 5" (Jadite: 30-35)		—	72-82	60-72
Relish Dish (oval, 2 sections)		—	13-15	10-12
Salt and Pepper 4" (footed)		—	52-58	42-52
Salt and Pepper 6"		—	—	44-55
Saucer		—	8-11	8-11
Sherbet		102-117	13-17	12-16
Sugar		70-87	12-15	10-13

ITEM	DESCRIPTION & REMARKS	DOLLAR VALUE RANGES BY COLOR		
		Delphite	Green	Pink
Sugar or Candy and cover		*74-88	31-37	24-30
Tray	6"	—	14-17	13-15
Tumbler	4½"	—	190-220	—
Tumbler	3½" (footed)	—	132-157	—
Tumbler	4" (footed)	—	18-23	18-23
Tumbler	4¾" (footed)	120-155	18-23	13-18
Tumbler	5¼" (footed)	—	36-46	36-46
Vase	(rose bowl, 3-legged)	—	440-510	—
Vase	(flared, 3-legged)	—	440-510	—
Vase	6 7/8"	—	435-515	—
Flower Frogs	(for vases)	—	6-9	—

* The Sugar or Candy COVER has not yet been seen in Delphite. It may or may not have been produced. If found this value would be much, much higher.

FLORAL and DIAMOND BAND

c. 1930

U. S. Glass Company

*Pittsburgh, Pennsylvania

Colors found to date:

- Black
- Blue
- Green
- Iridescent
- Pink

*The company had numerous locations for factories. Pittsburgh was one of the only two locations still operating in 1938.

FLORAL AND DIAMOND BAND

Reproductions or Reissues
None known to date.

General Pattern Notes
The collector should take particular note that there have been no cups and saucers found in this pattern and no evidence any were ever produced.

Green is the predominant color encountered, with pink following. The other colors should be considered fairly scarce and worth considerably more.

This is another pattern that has a heavy, quality feel unusual to typical depression glass items.

There is no significant difference between the pink and green items, although you might have to pay 10 - 20% more for the green.

ITEM	DESCRIPTION & REMARKS	DOLLAR VALUE RANGES BY COLOR
		Green or Pink
Bowl	4½"	6-9
Bowl	5¾" (handled)	9-12
Bowl	8"	12-16
Butter Dish and cover		96-111
Compote	5½"	11-15
Creamer	(small)	7-10
Creamer	4¾"	13-19
Pitcher	8"	95-120
Plate	8"	15-22
Sherbet		4-8
Sugar	(small)	7-10
Sugar and Cover	5¼"	39-55
Tumbler	4"	12-17
Tumbler	5"	21-27

FLORENTINE NUMBER ONE

1932 - 1935

Hazel Atlas Glass Company

Clarksburg, West Virginia and Zanesville, Ohio

FLORENTINE NO. 1. This drawing actually represents the pattern for FLORENTINE NO. 2 also. Please refer to the text of both pattern listings for an explanation of the difference.

Colors found to date:

- Cobalt
- Crystal
- Green
- Pink
- Yellow

FLORENTINE NUMBER ONE

Reproductions or Reissues

These are reproductions of the footed salt and pepper shakers to be found.

General Pattern Notes

This pattern is also frequently called "Old Florentine" and sometimes "Poppy No. 1".

Many of the items in the line are flanged and flat-rimmed with five distinct sides.

There is another quite similar pattern, "Florentine No. 2", on the following pages. The two patterns are easily confused by collectors, although the pattern on the Florentine No. 1 is very obviously rendered smaller than that of the No. 2 on the larger pieces. The chief difference to look for is that No. 1 has five-sided pieces and all the pieces in No. 2 are round and have no serrations. This is true regarding all pieces excepting the pitchers on which the patterns appear to be the same.

Blue (cobalt) pieces are the most rare.

ITEM	DESCRIPTION & REMARKS	DOLLAR VALUE RANGES BY COLOR		
		Crystal or Green	Pink	Yellow
Ash Tray	5½"	27-32	36-46	35-46
Bowl	5" (blue: 18-23)	10-12	12-15	10-13
Bowl	6"	12-15	15-19	14-16
Bowl	8½"	21-27	32-38	28-34
Bowl	9½" (oval, with cover)	42-52	55-67	55-64
Butter Dish and cover		154-189	205-255	165-205
Coaster or Ash Tray 3¾"		19-23	33-39	21-26
Creamer		11-13	14-18	14-16
Creamer	(ruffled edge) (blue: 60-75)	25-30	32-37	36-42
Cup		7-9	10-12	9-11
Pitcher	6½" (footed) (blue: 505-580)	45-56	55-67	60-70
Pitcher	7½"	60-70	154-190	170-200
Plate	6"	4-7	4-7	4-8
Plate	8½"	7-9	14-17	13-15
Plate	10"	12-15	21-26	18-23
Plate	10" (grill)	12-15	14-18	14-18
Platter	11½" (oval)	14-17	21-27	21-24
Salt and Pepper (footed)		36-43	66-75	60-70
Saucer		3-6	4-7	4-7
Sherbet	(footed)	6-9	12-15	11-13
Sugar and cover		26-30	14-16	11-13
Sugar	(ruffled edge)	26-30	18-23	18-23
Tumbler	3¼" (footed) (blue: 60-70)	12-15	28-35	32-37
Tumbler	3¾" (footed)	12-15	—	—
Tumbler	4¾" (footed)	15-21	19-25	19-25
Tumbler	5¼" (footed)	19-23	28-35	24-29
Tumbler	5¼"	—	32-37	30-35

FLORENTINE NUMBER TWO

1934 - 1937

Hazel Atlas Glass Company   Clarksburg, West Virginia and Zanesville, Ohio

Colors found to date:

- Amber (yellow)
  - Crystal
- Blue
- Green
- Blue (cobalt)
  - Pink

Reproductions or Reissues
None known to date.

General Pattern Notes
Please refer to Florentine No. 1 for pattern illustration and discussion of principal differences between these two patterns.

Footed pieces in Florentine No. 2 have round bases.

The two patterns mix together nicely, but many purist collectors wouldn't think of combining them.

Amber (yellow) and blue are the rare colors.

ITEM	DESCRIPTION & REMARKS	Crystal or Green	Pink	Yellow
Ash Tray	3¾"	18-23	—	29-35
Ash Tray	5½"	24-29	—	39-48
Bowl	4½"	12-14	14-17	20-23
Bowl	4¾" (cream soup)	14-16	14-16	20-24
Bowl	5" (blue: 35 - 45)	—	13-15	—
Bowl	5½"	23-27	—	36-42
Bowl	6"	18-23	23-27	31-38
Bowl	8"	23-27	27-32	26-30
Bowl	9" (oval, with cover)	42-52	—	60-71
Bowl	9"	25-30	—	—
Butter Dish and cover		120-150	—	160-205
Candlesticks	2¾" (pair)	47-58	—	52-65
Candy Dish and cover		105-117	156-188	177-214
Coaster	3¼"	13-16	23-27	24-30
Compote	3½" (ruffled edge) (blue: 66-76)	14-18	11-12	24-30
Creamer		11-12	—	11-13
Cup		8-10	—	11-12
Custard		41-48	—	59-71
Gravy Boat		—	—	50-61
Pitcher	6¼" (footed, cone shaped) (blue: 480-540)	—	—	132-157
Pitcher	7½" (footed, cone shaped)	29-36	—	29-35
Pitcher	8"	60-72	156-188	174-203
Plate	6"	3-6	—	3-7
Plate	6¼"	19-23	—	33-37
Plate	8½"	7-9	8-10	11-12

FLORENTINE NUMBER TWO

ITEM	DESCRIPTION & REMARKS	Crystal or Green	Pink	Yellow
Plate	10"	12-15	18-22	14-17
Plate	10¼" (grill)	10-12	—	12-14
Platter	11" (oval)	14-19	14-19	14-19
Platter	12" (for gravy boat)	—	—	45-55
Relish Dish	10" (3 sections)	12-15	24-28	21-26
Salt and Pepper	(pair)	45-57	—	57-68
Saucer		3-6	—	4-7
Sherbet	(footed)	10-12	—	12-15
Sugar and cover		21-26	—	31-37
Tray	(for shakers, creamer & sugar, round)	—	—	66-75
Tumbler	3½" (two styles)	11-16	13-16	21-26
Tumbler	4" (blue: 60 - 75)	14-16	14-16	21-25
Tumbler	5"	21-26	—	36-44
Tumbler	3¼" (footed)	12-15	—	13-15
Tumbler	4" (footed)	13-15	—	14-20
Tumbler	4½" (footed)	14-18	—	17-22
Tumbler	5" (footed)	21-26	—	36-45
Vase	6"	27-32	—	57-68

FLOWER GARDEN WITH BUTTERFLIES

1920's-1930's

U.S. Glass Company

Pittsburgh, Pennsylvania

Colors found to date:

- Amber
- Black
- Blue
- Crystal
- Green
- Pink
- Blue-green

Reproductions or Reissues
     None found to date
General Pattern Notes
     This pattern is also known as Butterflies and Roses. You may have to look hard to find the butterflies for they are relatively obscure. There is almost always at least one to be found somewhere in the design although it has been reported that it can be found without it altogether on rare occasions. This pattern is difficult to locate and the prices are rising at a phenominal rate. Rarest piece is the heart-shaped covered candy.

ITEM	DESCRIPTION OR REMARKS	VALUE RANGES BY COLOR
		All Colors
Ash Tray	has cigarette and match holders	195-218
Bowl	rolled edge, two types	82-107
Bowl	10", footed	88-108
Candlestick (pair) 4"		82-107
Candlestick (pair) 8"		99-138
Candy	8", covered	92-108
Candy	heart shape, covered	30-41
Cheese and Cracker plate, 10" and compote, 4"		77-97
Cigarette Box 3½" x 2½"		93-118
Cologne	7½" Footed, stoppered	195-220
Creamer		92-117
Cup		92-118
Mayonnaise 3 piece set		93-120
Plate	7"	17-22
Plate	8", two designs	22-27
Powder Jar		55-70
Powder Jar footed		120-140
Sandwich Plate, center handled		82-102
Saucer		44-64
Sugar	no cover	92-118
Tray	10" x 5½", oval	55-70
Tray	11¾" x 7¾", rectangular	70-85
Vase	6"	120-140
Vase	7"	120-140
Vase	10"	142-167

FOREST GREEN

1950s-1967

Anchor-Hocking Glass Corporation

Lancaster, Ohio
Long Island City, New York

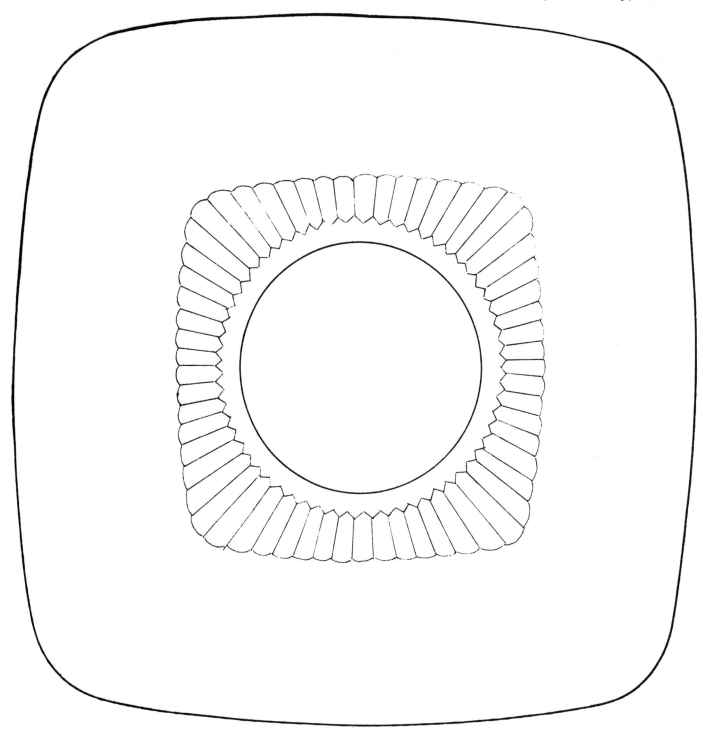

Colors found to date:

• Green only

FOREST GREEN

Reproductions or Reissues:
  None known to date
General Pattern Notes
  Although strictly speaking this is not Depression Era Glassware, Forest Green is very popular among collectors, hence, included here. It was introduced soon after Hocking Glass acquired the Anchor Cap and Closure Company and became Anchor-Hocking. The pattern utilized many of Hocking's molds for the older Royal Ruby pattern. As a general rule most of the pieces in both patterns are the same. The squared pieces were introduced much later than the others (see illustration accompanying). These squared pieces each have the ribbed design in the center. The other items have little or no ornamentation and are quite plain. The vibrant green and red (Royal Ruby) are the outstanding characteristics of both patterns.

ITEM	DESCRIPTION OR REMARKS	VALUE RANGES
Ash Tray		3-5
Bowl	4-¾"	3-6
Bowl	6"	7-10
Bowl	7¼"	7-10
Creamer		4-6
Cup		2-4
Mixing Bowls, 3 piece set		20-22
Mixing Bowls, no lip or spout		7-8
Pitcher	22 ounces	14-18
Pitcher	3 quart	24-28
Plate	6½"	2-4
Plate	8½"	4-6
Plate	10"	18-22
Platter	rectangular	22-25
Punch Bowl with stand		24-29
Punch Cup		2-4
Saucer		1-3
Sugar		4-6
Tumblers	2 sizes	2-6
Vase	Ball-type	3-5
Vase	6½"	3-6
Vase	9"	6-7

FORTUNE

1936 - 1938

Hocking Glass Company

(now Anchor-Hocking Glass Corporation)

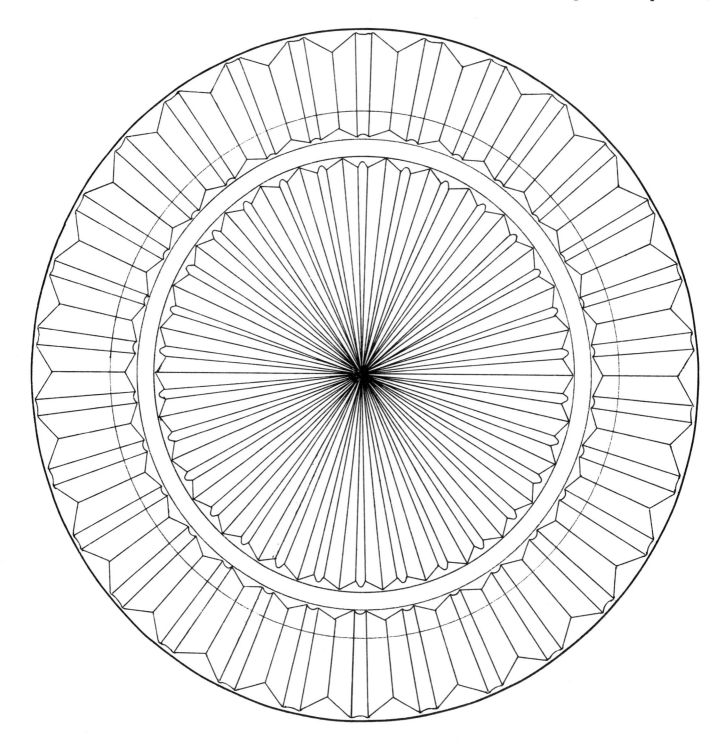

Colors found to date:

- Crystal
- Pink

FORTUNE

Reproductions or Reissues
    None known to date.

General Pattern Notes
    Made as a cereal promotion pattern, there are not many pieces out there and available to collectors. The eight-inch luncheon plates are the most difficult to locate.

ITEM	DESCRIPTION & REMARKS	DOLLAR VALUE RANGES BY COLOR
		Crystal or Pink
Bowl	4"	3-6
Bowl	4½"	4-7
Bowl	4½" (handled)	4-7
Bowl	5¼" (rolled edge)	6-8
Bowl	7¾"	7-9
Candy Dish and cover		19-25
Cup		4-7
Plate	6"	3-6
Plate	8"	6-8
Saucer		3-6
Tumbler	3½"	4-7
Tumbler	4"	6-8

FRUITS

1930's

Manufacture attributed to several companies.

FRUITS. Saucer.
Larger pieces have the
cherry motif repeated in the center.

Colors found to date:

- Crystal
- Green
- Pink

FRUITS

Reproductions or Reissues
    None known to date.

General Pattern Notes
    This is a pattern that is simple and attractive. Few pieces are known to exist; eleven types in all.
    Because Fruits was made by several different companies, the fruits may vary somewhat and in the case of some of the tumblers, there are some very desirable ones that bear the cherry motif only. There have been reports of some iridescent pieces surfacing.

ITEM	DESCRIPTION & REMARKS	DOLLAR VALUE RANGES BY COLOR
		Green or Pink
Bowl	5"	16-21
Bowl	8"	46-58
Cup		6-8
Pitcher	7"	54-64
Plate	8"	6-8
Saucer		3-6
Sherbet		8-10
Tumbler	3½"	12-16
Tumbler	4" (cherries or pears only)	14-18
Tumbler	4"	12-16
Tumbler	5"	31-37

GEORGIAN

1931 - 1936

Federal Glass Company

Columbus, Ohio

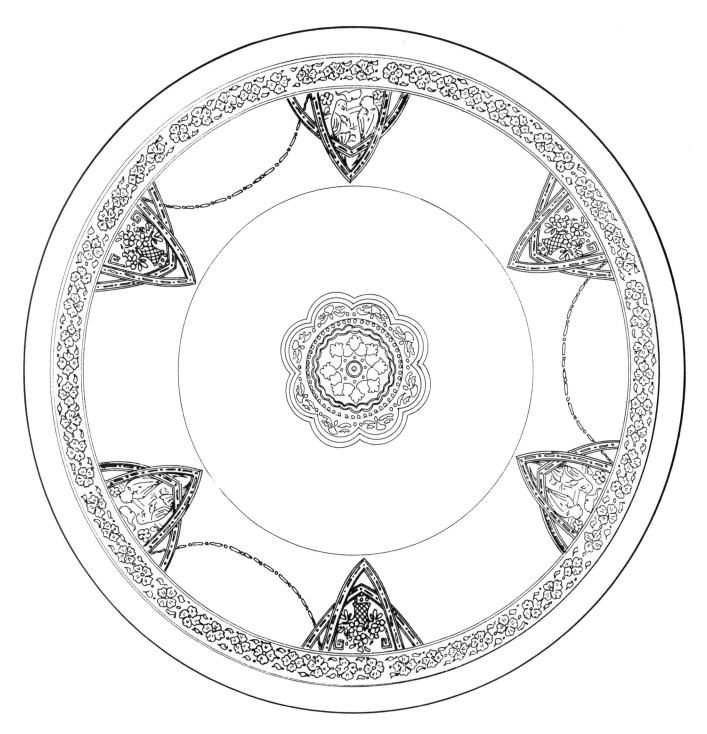

Colors found to date:

• Crystal   • Green

Reproductions or Reissues
None known to date.

General Pattern Notes
This pattern is also popularly known as "Love Birds".

An unusual piece to be found is the wooden lazy susan, 18¼ inches. It has 7 sections in which the 6-inch hot plate dishes are to be placed. A complete set of the lazy susan and plates would be valued in the mid to high hundreds of dollars.

Dinner plates are found with the full design and also with the edge design (no center design and no love birds or baskets). The tumblers exhibit baskets only in the design and the lids of the sugars have only the edge design present. The other covered pieces have complete lid designs.

ITEM	DESCRIPTION & REMARKS	DOLLAR VALUE RANGES BY COLOR
		Green
Bowl	4½"	7-9
Bowl	5¾"	14-20
Bowl	6½"	63-75
Bowl	7½"	60-70
Bowl	9" (oval)	63-74
Butter Dish and cover		100-115
Creamer	3" (footed)	12-17
Creamer	4" (footed)	14-20
Cup		12-14
Hot Plate	5" (center design)	45-58
Plate	6"	6-7
Plate	8"	9-12
Plate	9¼"	25-34
Plate	9¼" (center design)	21-28
Platter	11½" (closed handles)	60-75
Saucer		4-6
Sherbet		13-16
Sugar and cover 3" (footed)		30-37
Sugar and cover 4" (footed)		45-55
Tumbler	4"	45-57
Tumbler	5¼"	63-75

HARP

1950's

Jeanette Glass Company

Jeanette, Pennsylvania

Colors found to date:
- Crystal
- Light Blue
- Crystal with Gold rims

Reproductions and Reissues:
    None known to date
Pattern Notes
    Little is known about the number of pieces to be found in this pattern. It appears to be limited as you may note from the listing below. It looks as if it might have been made only as a party or hostess set due to the small number and type of pieces that have so far been found.

ITEM	DESCRIPTION AND REMARKS	DOLLAR VALUE RANGES
		Crystal
Ash Tray-Coaster combination, 4¾" x 3¼"		6-7
Coaster		3-5
Cup		4-8
Saucer		3-5
Cake Stand	9" high	17-22
Plate	7¼"	6-7
Tray	rectangular	20-28
Vase	6"	11-16

Key For Cover Photos

GREEN	TOPAZ or YELLOW	ULTRAMARINE	AMBER (Light)
CREMAX	FOREST GREEN	PINK	FROSTED or PINK SATIN FINISH
PINK (Orange Cast)	MONAX	COBALT	GREEN OPALESCENT

FRONT COVER

BACK COVER

CRYSTAL	RUBY RED	CRYSTAL on METAL BASE	IRIDESCENT
JADITE	LIGHT BLUE	DELPHITE	AMETHYST
SHELL PINK	AMBER (Dark)	OPALESCENT	IRIDESCENT

HERITAGE

c. 1940's

Federal Glass Company

Columbus, Ohio

Colors found to date:

- Blue
- Crystal
- Green
- Pink

Reproductions or Reissues
None are known to date.

General Pattern Notes
The crystal is the most common with the other colors only occasionally being found. From time to time the collector may find some with gold edge trim.

Values for pink are about three times and blue and green are roughly five times the values for crystal listed below.

ITEM	DESCRIPTION & REMARKS	DOLLAR VALUE RANGES BY COLOR
		Crystal
Bowl	5"	6-8
Bowl	8½"	18-23
Bowl	10½"	17-21
Cup		3-6
Creamer	(footed)	14-19
Plate	8"	6-8
Plate	9¼"	8-10
Plate	12"	21-14
Saucer		3-6
Sugar	(footed)	14-17

HEX OPTIC or HONEYCOMB

1928 - 1932

Federal Glass Company

Columbus, Ohio

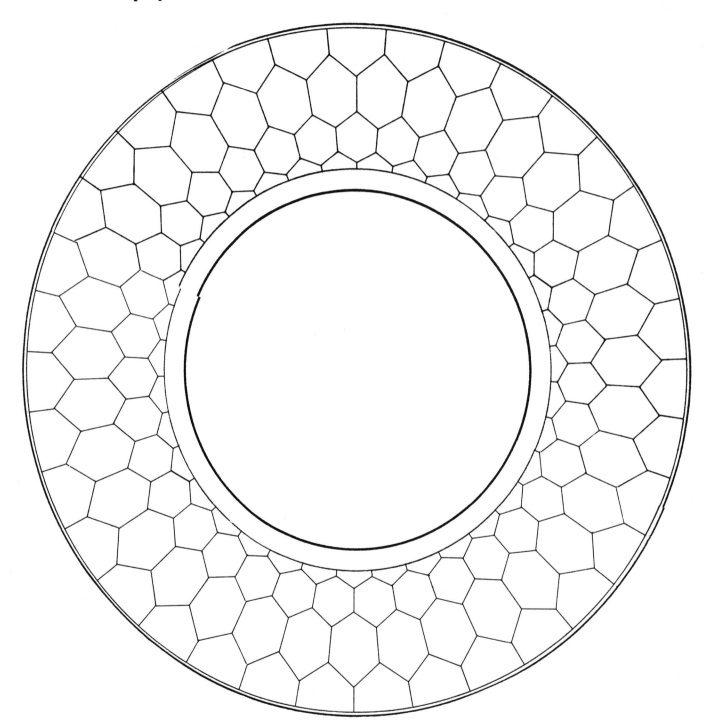

Colors found to date:

- Green
- Pink

HEX OPTIC or HONEYCOMB

Reproductions or Reissues
    None known to date.

General Pattern Notes
    Known by both names above about equally although "Hex Optic" is also used as a generic term to describe a **type** of pattern made by many different companies. "Honeycomb" is therefore preferable.
    Tumblers and pitchers appeared in iridescent in the 1960's.
    May have been made by other companies also.

ITEM	DESCRIPTION & REMARKS	DOLLAR VALUE RANGES BY COLOR
		Green or Pink
Bowl	4¼"	3-6
Bowl	7½"	7-10
Bowl	7¼"	5-10
Bowl	8¼"	10-12
Bowl	9"	11-13
Bowl	10"	13-17
Ice Bucket		26-31
Butter Dish and cover (rectangular)		25-29
Creamer	(2 styles)	4-7
Cup	(2 styles)	3-6
Ice Bucket	(metal handle)	11-14
Pitcher	5" (sunflower in bottom)	46-54
Pitcher	9" (footed)	35-44
Plate	6"	2-5
Plate	8"	5-9
Platter	11"	6-10
Refrigerator Dish 4"		5-8
Refrigerator Stack Set (3 pieces)		38-43
Salt and Pepper (pair)		23-28
Saucer		2-5
Sugar	(2 styles)	4-8
Sherbet	5 oz. (footed)	4-7
Tumbler	3¾"	4-8
Tumbler	5¾" (footed)	5-8
Tumbler	7" (footed)	6-10
Whiskey Jigger 2"		4-7

HOBNAIL

1934 - 1936

Hocking Glass Company   (now Anchor-Hocking Glass Corporation)

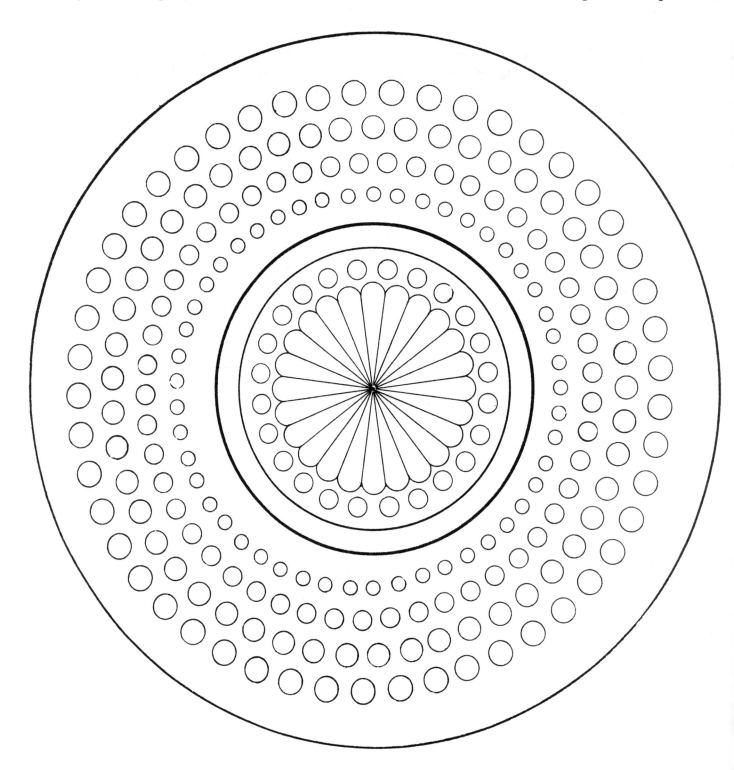

Colors found to date:

• Crystal   • Pink

HOBNAIL

Reproductions or Reissues
    None known.

General Pattern Notes
    Collectors should be aware that the "Moonstone" pattern, found on later pages in this book, is virtually the same pattern design with a few additions of ornament and some different type pieces.
    Crystal is the most common of the two colors with the pink being relatively scarce.
    There are some crystal pieces with a very attractive red edge trim. This apparently is present only on luncheon sets.
    Hobnail was made in some of the old molds as far as is known, into the late 1960's. These are all in opaque white.

ITEM	DESCRIPTION & REMARKS	DOLLAR VALUE RANGES BY COLOR
		Crystal or Pink
Bowl	5½"	3-6
Bowl	7"	2-5
Cup		3-6
Creamer	(footed)	3-6
Decanter and Stopper		20-25
Goblet	10 oz.	6-9
Goblet	13 oz.	7-10
Pitcher	18 oz.	17-20
Pitcher		24-29
Plate	6"	2-5
Plate	8½"	2-5
Saucer		2-5
Sherbet		3-6
Sugar	(footed)	3-6
Tumbler	5 oz.	4-7
Tumbler	9 oz.	6-9
Tumbler	10 oz.	7-10
Tumbler	15 oz.	7-10
Tumbler	3 oz. (footed)	6-8
Tumbler	5 oz. (footed)	6-8
Whiskey Jigger 1½ oz.		6-8

HOLIDAY
1947 - 1949

Jeannette Glass Company

Jeannette, Pennsylvania

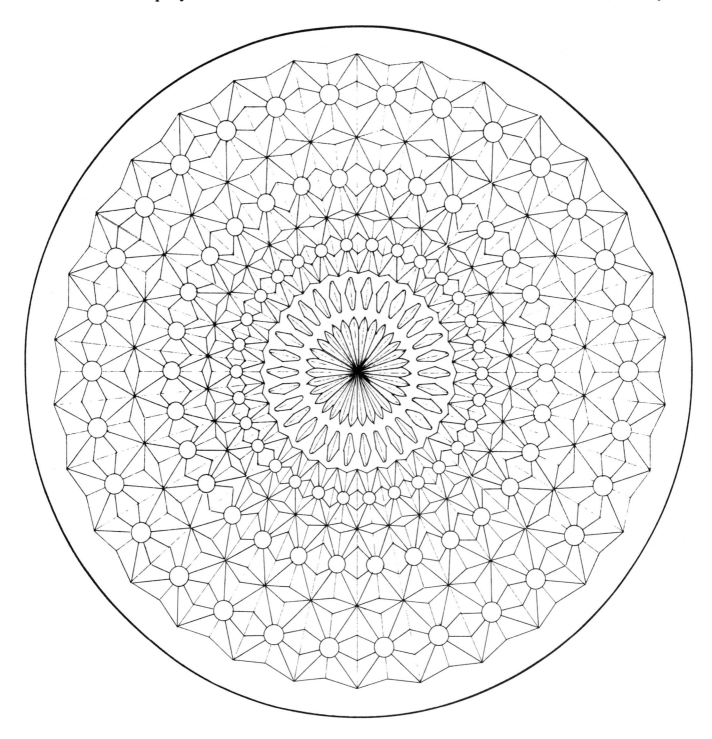

Colors found to date:

- Crystal
- Pink
- Shell Pink
- White (opaque)

Reproductions or Reissues

None known

General Pattern Notes

A very intricate geometric design that flows nicely in spite of the straight lines and acute angles. This pattern is also known as "Buttons and Bows".

Pink is by far the most commonly found and collected color in the pattern. Some white and iridescent pieces were produced in the later days of manufacture and a shell pink piece was also offered. The latter, a console, and 16-ounce milk pitchers are considered very desirable by the collector, but the shell pink is an elusive catch.

There are two different types of cups to be found in Holiday.

ITEM	DESCRIPTION & REMARKS	DOLLAR VALUE RANGES BY COLOR
		Pink
Bowl	5 1/8"	8-10
Bowl	7¾"	32-41
Bowl	8½"	24-28
Bowl	9½" (oval)	15-21
Bowl	10¾" (console)	95-118
Butter Dish and cover		45-56
Cake Plate	10½" (3-legged)	78-94
Candlesticks 3" (pair)		76-90
Creamer	(footed)	8-11
Cup	(2 sizes)	7-8
Pitcher	4¾"	55-67
Pitcher	6¾"	37-44
Plate	6"	3-6
Plate	9"	12-15
Plate	13¾" (salver)	90-103
Platter	11 3/8" (oval)	14-17
Sandwich Tray 10½"		13-15
Saucer	(2 styles)	3-6
Sherbet		6-9
Sugar and cover		16-21
Tumbler	4"	19-24
Tumbler	4" (footed)	42-51
Tumbler	6" (footed)	81-95

HOMESPUN
1938 - 1940

Jeannette Glass Company

Jeannette, Pennsylvania

Colors found to date:

• Crystal

• Pink

HOMESPUN

Reproductions or Reissues
None known to date.

General Pattern Notes
A very rare, large (96-ounce) pitcher exists in this pattern. A significant identifying characteristic of its design is that it does not have the characteristic waffle-like center design, only the fine ribbing design.

Another significant item is the tea set. The entire set of 14 pieces would bring around $350.00 or more, this especially if it were to be found in the original packing box. The set is called "Homespun Tea Set". It is often referred to as a child's tea set. The **crystal** teapot is very rare. In fact no one knows of one in a collection, but since the company advertised the sets as available in both colors, there is good reason to believe some lucky collector will eventually discover this treasure. Keep your eyeballs peeled and moving all the time on your hunts!

ITEM	DESCRIPTION & REMARKS	DOLLAR VALUE RANGES BY COLOR
		Crystal or Pink
Bowl	4½" (closed handles)	6-8
Bowl	5"	12-15
Bowl	8¼"	13-17
Butter Dish and cover		60-70
Coaster or Ash Tray		6-9
Creamer	(footed)	10-12
Cup		4-7
Pitcher		44-53
Plate	6"	3-6
Plate	9¼"	12-15
Platter	13" (closed handles)	12-15
Saucer		3-6
Sherbet		8-10
Sugar	(footed)	9-12
Tumbler	4"	10-13
Tumbler	5¼"	22-26
Tumbler	4" (footed)	12-14
Tumbler	6¼" (footed)	14-16
Tumbler	6½" (footed)	21-27

HORSESHOE (No. 612)

1930 - 1933

Indiana Glass Company   **Dunkirk, Indiana**

Colors to be found:

- Crystal   • Green   • Pink   • Yellow

HORSESHOE (No. 612)

Reproductions or Reissues
None known to date.

General Pattern Notes
To find crystal pieces in Horseshoe would be an exciting event indeed. They are so scarce that there is not sufficient trade data even to establish value, but it would be high compared to the rest of the pattern values.

Other rare pieces are the butter dish with cover, the pitcher, the covered candy dish with metal holder, and the grill plates.

There are some items without the center design. These are the candy dish (design on cover) and some of the plates.

ITEM	DESCRIPTION & REMARKS	DOLLAR VALUE RANGES BY COLOR	
		Green	Yellow
Bowl	4½"	24-30	20-27
Bowl	6½"	16-22	22-29
Bowl	7½"	20-24	22-30
Bowl	8½"	23-28	33-39
Bowl	9½"	34-42	36-46
Bowl	10½" (oval)	19-24	24-32
Butter Dish and cover		590-700	—
Candy and cover with metal holder		154-220	—
Creamer	(footed)	15-21	15-21
Cup		10-14	10-14
Pitcher	8½"	236-305	245-320
Plate	6"	3-6	7-9
Plate	8 3/8"	7-10	10-13
Plate	9 3/8"	11-13	11-14
Plate	10 3/8"	20-27	22-31
Plate	10 3/8" (grill)	25-32	25-31
Plate	11"	13-17	16-20
Platter	10¾" (oval)	20-24	23-28
Relish	(footed, 3 sections)	15-19	19-24
Saucer		4-7	4-7
Sherbet		13-19	16-20
Sugar	(no cover)	13-19	13-18
Tumbler	4¼"	90-106	—
Tumbler	4¾"	96-113	—
Tumbler	9 oz. (footed)	17-23	19-25
Tumbler	12 oz. (footed)	84-98	96-113

IRIS

1928 - 1932

Jeannette Glass Company

Jeannette, Pennsylvania

IRIS. There is always a
"herringbone" type background pattern
to be found with this design. For example, in this drawing
the herringbone is within the herringbone border drawn around the flowers and
extends fully behind them. The herringbone is also found behind border designs when present.

Colors found to date:

- Amber (iridescent)   • Blue (light)   • Crystal   • Pink

Reproductions or Reissues

There were some iridescent pieces of Iris issued in 1950 and in 1969. Whether to call these reissues is a hazy proposition, but the production of crystal in 1969 can be called reissue, as well as a candy dish (no lid) released in 1970 in white. Reissues of the vases can be identified by the iridescent color and the candy dish reissue has no design on the bottom as the old ones do. These are the most recent reissues.

General Pattern Notes

The 1928-32 original releases were in crystal with some odd pieces in pink. Note the design drawing on the previous page does not illustrate the fine line herringbone background that is always present.

The 7½ inch soup bowl in crystal has become quite scarce and is considered fairly rare these days.

Coasters are quite rare and some items have appeared frosted.

ITEM	DESCRIPTION & REMARKS	DOLLAR VALUE RANGES BY COLOR	
		Crystal	Iridescent (amber)
Bowl	4½" (beaded edge)	33-39	8-12
Bowl	5"	15-20	8-14
Bowl	5" (ruffled edge)	7-10	7-8
Bowl	6"	33-39	—
Bowl	7½"	113-133	31-40
Bowl	8" (ruffled edge)	17-24	17-23
Bowl	8" (beaded edge)	50-63	18-23
Bowl	9½"	14-17	13-17
Bowl	11" (ruffled edge)	15-19	11-15
Bowl	11"	41-48	—
Butter Dish and cover		44-50	51-64
Candlesticks (pair)		26-36	37-43
Candy Jar and cover		79-103	—
Coaster		50-63	—
Creamer (footed)		7-10	8-12
Cup		13-17	13-17
Demitasse Cup		24-32	44-55
Demitasse Saucer		37-43	66-81
Fruit or Nut Set		45-56	—
Goblet	4"	19-23	21-27
Goblet	4½"	19-24	—
Goblet	5¾" (two styles)	17-28	—
Pitcher	9½" (footed)	32-40	42-49
Plate	5½"	7-10	6-8
Plate	8"	49-63	—
Plate	9"	42-52	27-34
Plate	11¾"	15-21	15-22
Saucer		6-8	6-8
Sherbet	2½" (footed)	18-21	10-14
Sherbet	4" (footed)	14-17	—
Sugar and cover		18-22	20-25
Tumbler	4"	50-64	—
Tumbler	6" (footed)	15-21	16-22
Tumbler	7" (footed)	21-28	21-27
Vase	9"	22-28	22-28

JUBILEE

1920's-1930's

Lancaster Glass Company

Lancaster, Ohio

JUBILEE

Reproductions or Reissues
  None known to date

General Pattern Notes
  Although, as noted above, there are no reproductions or reissues in this pattern, there are several very similar pieces to be found. The principal differences are that the similar patterns have alternating large small petals and the centers of the flowers frequently have design detail while Jubilee has void centers and the petals are more uniform in size. The designs are otherwise so similar that the non-Jubilee items mix and match well.
  The pattern color is predominantly yellow, but a very few pieces have been found in pink.
  The rarest item to be found is the three piece mayonnaise set consisting of plate, bowl and serving spoon. The spoon is seldom found.

ITEM	DESCRIPTION & REMARKS	DOLLAR VALUE RANGES BY COLOR
		Yellow
Bowl	9" (handled)	100-125
Candle Holder (pair)		135-150
Cheese and cracker set		125-140
Creamer		19-21
Sugar		19-22
Cup		14-16
Saucer		3-5
Goblet	10 Oz., 6"	26-29
Goblet	12½ Oz., 6-⅛"	30-33
Mayonnaise set (3 pieces)		200-215
	without the serving spoon	180-200
Plate	7"	7-9
Plate	8¾"	9-11
Plate	13"	24-28
Sherbet	4¾"	8-10
Tray	11' (2-handled)	24-26
Tray	(center-handled)	100-125

LACE EDGE

1935 - 1938

Hocking Glass Company

(now Anchor-Hocking Glass Corporation)

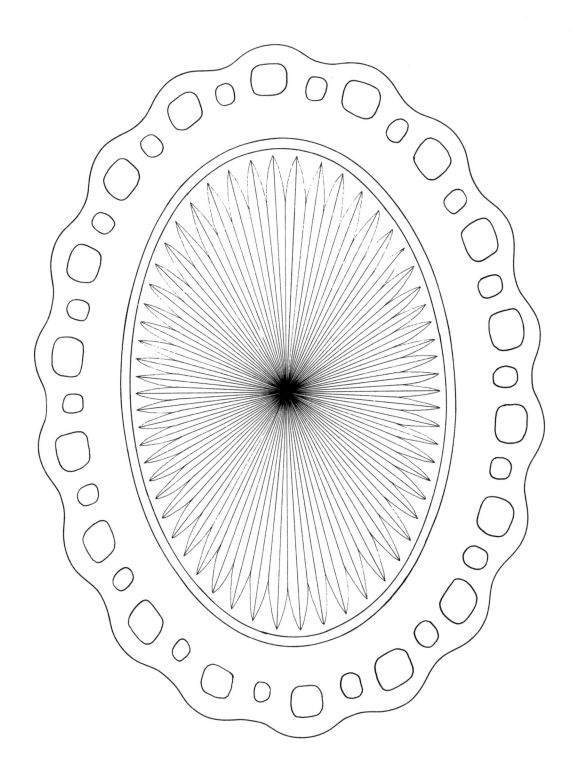

Colors found to date:

• Crystal   • Pink

Reproductions or Reissues
None known to date.

General Pattern Notes
The characteristic lace edge of this pattern is not utilized on cups, creamers, sugars or tumblers.
Hocking made this pattern mostly in pink with just a few in crystal. Other companies made items much like Lace Edge in other colors, so don't confuse them.
Hocking also made some of these pieces in a "frosted" or "satin" finish. These are worth only about 50% of those listed below.

ITEM	DESCRIPTION & REMARKS	DOLLAR VALUE RANGES BY COLOR
		Pink
Bowl	6 3/8"	12-16
Bowl	7¾"	18-24
Bowl	9½" (plain or ribbed)	17-20
Bowl	10½" (3-legged)	150-190
Butter Dish or Bon Bon Dish with cover		70-83
Candlesticks (pair)		150-190
Candy Jar and cover (ribbed)		45-69
Compote	7" (footed)	17-21
Compote and cover (footed)		85-101
Cookie Jar and cover		55-64
Creamer		18-21
Cup		19-23
Fish Bowl, ½ gal., 1 gal., 2 gal., (crystal only: 54-70)		—
Flower Bowl (with crystal frog)		26-32
Plate	7¼"	15-19
Plate	8¾"	15-19
Plate	10½"	25-30
Plate	10½" (grill)	15-19
Plate	10½" Relish (3 sections)	25-29
Plate	13" (solid lace, 4 sections)	21-25
Platter	12¾"	25-30
Platter	12¾" (5 sections)	23-27
Relish Dish	7½" (3 sections)	44-52
Saucer		9-11
Sherbet	(footed)	54-67
Sugar		15-19
Tumbler	3½"	11-13
Tumbler	4½"	12-15
Tumbler	5"	45-57
Vase	7"	240-290

LINCOLN INN
c. 1930

Fenton Art Glass Company   Williamstown, West Virginia

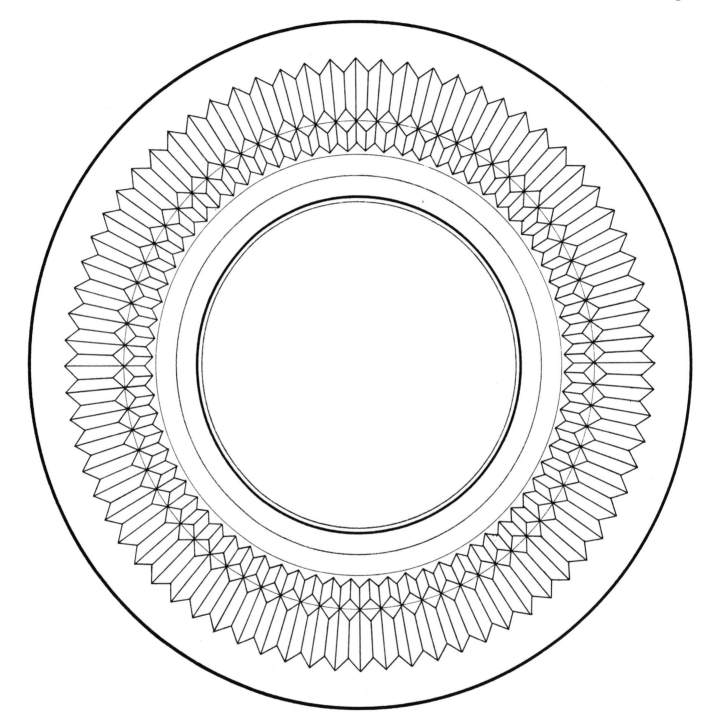

Colors in this pattern:

- Amethyst
- Aquamarine
- Black
- Blue
- Cobalt or Royal Blue
- Crystal
- Green
- Jade (translucent)
- Pink
- Red
- Yellow

Reproductions or Reissues
None known to date.

General Pattern Notes
Advertising indicates the first release of this pattern by Fenton was in 1928. Colors noted on previous page may or may not have been found. They are taken from several references and from old Fenton advertising.

This is fine quality glass, much of it handmade. It is not, strictly speaking, depression glass, but it is of the same era.

Salt and pepper shakers seem to be the most elusive pieces in the pattern.

ITEM	DESCRIPTION & REMARKS	DOLLAR VALUE RANGES BY COLOR	
		Blue or Red	Other Colors
Ash Tray		15-17	5-8
Bon Bon	(square)	15-17	10-12
Bon Bon	(oval)	15-17	10-12
Bowl	5"	7-10	4-7
Bowl	6"	11-13	5-9
Bowl	6" (crimped edge)	13-15	6-10
Bowl, Olive	(with handle)	13-15	6-10
Bowl, Finger		11-14	10-12
Bowl	9¼" (footed)	18-24	14-17
Bowl	10½" (footed)	25-32	18-22
Candy Dish	(footed, oval)	14-17	10-12
Compote		12-14	6-10
Creamer		22-26	14-18
Cup		13-17	10-12
Goblet, water		22-28	14-17
Goblet, wine		17-21	12-14
Nut Dish	(footed)	14-17	10-11
Pitcher	7¼"	—	315-380
Plate	6"	4-7	3-6
Plate	8"	8-10	4-7
Plate	9¼"	10-14	7-10
Plate	12"	18-23	13-15
Salt and Pepper (pair)		165-205	100-135
Saucer		3-6	2-5
Sherbet	4¾"	17-22	10-13
Sugar		22-27	15-19
Tumbler	4 oz.	14-18	10-11
Tumbler	5 oz. (footed)	16-20	11-13
Tumbler	7 oz. (footed)	17-21	11-13
Tumbler	9 oz. (footed)	20-23	13-15
Tumbler	12 oz. (footed)	22-28	13-17
Vase	12" (footed)	88-100	52-65

LORAIN

1929 - 1932

Indiana Glass Company

Dunkirk, Indiana

Colors found to date:

- Crystal
- Green
- Yellow

Reproductions or Reissues
None known to date.

General Pattern Notes
Yellow is the most frequently found color but difficult to obtain insofar as a complete set is concerned.

One of the rarer items to be found is the 10¼ inch dinner plate in yellow and the larger dinner plates are thought to be non-existent.

Rarer still is the deep 8 inch bowl.

The pattern is sometimes known as "Basket".

ITEM	DESCRIPTION & REMARKS	DOLLAR VALUE RANGES BY COLOR	
		Crystal or Green	Yellow
Bowl	6"	33-38	60-70
Bowl	7¼"	36-44	56-64
Bowl	8"	98-106	140-167
Bowl	9¾" (oval)	36-44	58-70
Creamer	(footed)	17-20	26-32
Cup		12-15	13-18
Plate	5½"	4-8	6-10
Plate	7¾"	11-13	17-20
Plate	8 3/8"	21-26	33-38
Plate	10¼"	36-43	56-69
Platter	11½"	27-33	40-48
Relish	8" (4 sections)	19-23	33-38
Saucer		5-7	5-7
Sherbet	(footed)	21-24	38-44
Snack Tray		15-20	—
Sugar	(footed)	16-20	21-27
Tumbler	4¾" (footed)	21-24	26-33

MADRID
1932 - 1939

Federal Glass Company

Columbus, Ohio

Colors found to date:

- Amber
- Blue
- Crystal
- Green
- Pink

MADRID

Reproductions or Reissues

Madrid has been reissued twice, once by Federal and later by another company.

The first reissue was by Federal in commemoration of the Bicentennial and easily identified by the presence of a small "76" molded into the back of each piece. All these were issued in amber. There are a total of 14 pieces in this Bicentennial set. The amber color is darker than that on the old original issue.

There have been a few butter dish tops to appear in crystal, some with the "76" and some without it. These were probably a trial run so they are limited.

In 1982 the Indiana Glass Company, who had bought Federal's molds, reissued practically the entire line in crystal.

General Pattern Notes

The first color this pattern was made in was green, followed a year or so later with amber.

The green was phased out and amber became the predominant color in which the pattern was made. Blue and pink were added but neither color remained in production long.

The larger size pitchers in crystal, amber and green are highly sought items, but the prize is the lazy susan in wood with the seven hot plate coasters fitted.

Cups are found with the ribbing inside or out.

ITEM	DESCRIPTION & REMARKS	DOLLAR VALUE RANGES BY COLOR			
		Blue	Crystal or Amber	Green	Pink
Ash Tray	(square)	—	155-189	114-135	—
Bowl	4¾" (cream soup)	—	11-14	7-11	7-11
Bowl	5"	10-12	6-9	13-16	—
Bowl	7"	15-17	11-14	23-28	—
Bowl	8"	29-36	14-18	—	26-32
Bowl	9 3/8"	—	20-24	—	—
Bowl	9½"	—	26-32	20-23	16-22
Bowl	10" (oval)	26-33	15-19	—	11-13
Bowl	11" (low console)	—	13-16	93-110	—
Butter Dish and cover		—	88-96	—	20-24
Candlesticks 2¼" (pair)		—	21-25	—	30-38
Cookie Jar and cover		—	38-50	12-14	—
Creamer	(footed)	13-17	9-10	9-10	9-10
Cup		13-17	6-10	7-11	12-14
Gravy Boat and drip plate		—	975-1040	—	—
Hot Dish Coaster		—	37-45	40-50	—
Jam Dish	7"	29-36	23-28	20-23	—
Jello Mold	2 1/8"	—	10-12	—	—
Pitcher	5½"	—	36-45	—	—
Pitcher	8"	167-210	40-49	143-175	44-54
Pitcher	8½"	—	66-81	210-235	—
Pitcher	8½" (ice lip)	—	66-81	210-235	—
Plate	6"	8-10	3-6	3-6	4-7

ITEM	DESCRIPTION & REMARKS	DOLLAR VALUE RANGES BY COLOR			
		Blue	Crystal or Amber	Green	Pink
Plate	7½"	16-21	11-14	12-14	12-15
Plate	8 7/8"	17-22	5-8	12-14	7-10
Plate	10½"	49-63	33-41	35-43	33-41
Plate	10½" (grill)	—	11-14	20-24	—
Plate	10¼" (relish)	—	11-14	13-17	12-15
Plate	11¼" (cake)	—	13-15	25-30	13-15
Platter	11½" (oval)	23-28	13-16	16-21	13-16
Salt and Pepper	3½" (footed)	140-183	77-91	104-130	—
Salt and Pepper	3½"	—	49-63	82-94	—
Saucer		5-8	3-6	4-7	3-6
Sherbet	(2 styles)	13-16	7-11	10-12	—
Sugar and cover		90-105	41-54	48-56	—
Tumbler	3 7/8"	24-28	15-19	38-48	—
Tumbler	4¼"	24-29	14-18	25-30	16-22
Tumbler	5½"	26-33	22-27	33-40	—
Tumbler	4" (footed)	—	22-27	55-65	—
Tumbler	5½" (footed)	—	26-32	38-48	—
Wooden Lazy Susan with 7 small hot dish coasters		—	575-650	—	—

MANHATTAN

1938 - 1941

Anchor-Hocking Glass Corporation

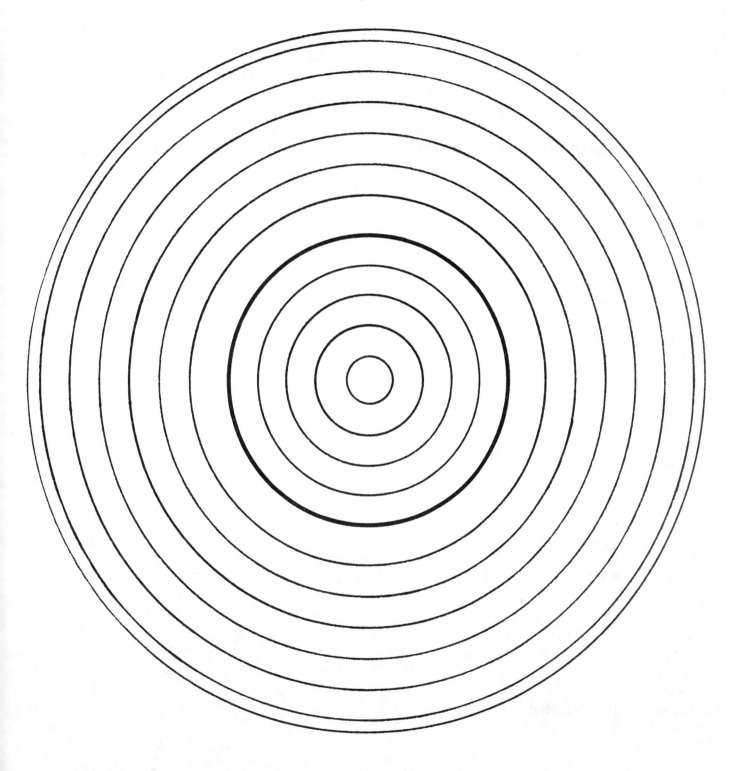

Colors found to date:

- Crystal
- Green
- Pink
- Red (Ruby Red)

MANHATTAN

Reproductions or Reissues
None known to date.

General Pattern Notes
The green seems to edge out the other colors in amount available. The ruby red and pink are not seen often and the crystal, which follows pink in availability, was introduced in 1940.

One of the most popular items in this pattern line is the 5-section relish tray with contrasting colored inserts. The round tilted pitcher remains a favorite also.

ITEM	DESCRIPTION & REMARKS	DOLLAR VALUE RANGES BY COLOR	
		Crystal	Pink
Ash Tray		10-13	—
Bowl	4½"	6-9	8-11
Bowl	5 3/8" (handled)	6-8	7-9
Bowl	7½"	8-12	8-12
Bowl	8" (closed handles)	14-18	14-18
Bowl	9"	12-15	14-17
Bowl	9½"	21-25	24-29
Candlesticks	4½" (pair)	12-15	—
Candy Dish	(3 legged)	4-7	8-11
Candy Dish and cover		25-30	—
Coaster		3-7	3-7
Compote	5¾"	11-15	11-15
Cookie Jar		13-15	19-25
Creamer		4-7	7-9
Cup		10-13	130-150
Relish Tray	14" (4 sections)	11-13	14-16
Relish Tray	14" (5 sections)	13-15	21-27
Relish Tray Insert		4-8	4-8
Pitcher	42 oz.	22-26	36-42
Pitcher	80 oz. (tilted)	26-32	45-58
Plate	6"	3-6	30-35
Plate	8½"	7-10	7-10
Plate	10¼"	15-20	75-100
Plate	14"	12-15	12-15
Salt and Pepper	2" (pair)	18-23	39-49
Saucer		3-6	—
Sherbet		7-10	7-10
Sugar		4-7	8-10
Tumbler	10 oz. (footed)	11-15	11-15
Vase	8"	11-13	—
Wine Glass		11-13	—

MAYFAIR

1934

Federal Glass Company

Columbus, Ohio

Colors found to date:

- Amber
- Crystal
- Green

MAYFAIR

Reproductions or Reissues
    None known to date.

General Pattern Notes
    A pattern which is in short supply, Mayfair was discontinued soon after production began. It seems that Federal tried to register the name with their design copyright only to find out that the "Mayfair" name had already been registered to another company. Subsequently they removed it from production. After some experimentation with design changes they had reworked the molds to the "Rosemary" design. The resulting design transition pieces are usually lumped in with one or the other, but they are really neither. Interesting they are but should be considered oddities, the collection of which is entirely up to the collector's disposition.

ITEM	DESCRIPTION & REMARKS	DOLLAR VALUE RANGES BY COLOR		
		Amber	Crystal	Green
Bowl	5"	4-8	4-8	6-10
Bowl	5" (cream soup)	17-24	12-16	17-22
Bowl	6"	17-22	9-13	18-24
Bowl	10" (oval)	17-24	12-16	18-24
Creamer	(footed)	12-16	11-14	12-15
Cup		6-11	4-8	9-12
Plate	6¾"	4-7	3-6	5-9
Plate	9½"	12-17	9-12	12-15
Plate	9½" (grill)	12-16	10-13	10-14
Platter	12" (oval)	17-22	12-16	18-24
Saucer		3-6	2-5	3-6
Sugar	(footed)	12-16	10-14	12-16
Tumbler	4½"	13-17	9-12	17-23

MAYFAIR (OPEN ROSE)

1931 - 1937

Hocking Glass Company   (Now Anchor-Hocking Glass Corporation)

Colors found to date:

- Blue
- Pink
- Crystal
- Green
- Yellow

MAYFAIR (OPEN ROSE)

Reproductions or Reissues

Until recently it was thought there were reproductions of only the whisky jiggers. They first surfaced in 1978 and can be found in pink, green and blue. The identification of the reproduction jigger in green and blue is easy for the original was not made in either color. The pink might cause you some trouble if you can't compare with a known original. It has been reported that the reproductions all have incomplete pattern design and their bases are thicker.

There are now reproductions of the salt and pepper shakers and the cookie jar.

General Pattern Notes

This is the "Mayfair" pattern that resulted in Federal discontinuing their own Mayfair pattern when they discovered that Hocking had already registered the name. There is no similarity of design.

Also called "Open Rose" by some. this is one of the most popularly collected patterns of depression era glassware.

Mayfair was originally released in pink. The original line had more than 50 items in it. Soon after came the blue and some pieces of green. Only a very modest number of pieces were made in crystal and along with the scarcity of crystal goes yellow.

Rarest of the pieces in this collection are the three-leg, nine-inch bowl, the pair of footed salt and pepper shakers, both in pink, and pink, green or yellow footed sugars **with lid**. Whiskey jiggers appear in pink only. There are some items that have been found with a frosted finish and the flower mold design around the border has been painted in realistic colors. There are several others that will require the extraction of a tooth or two in terms of money required for acquisition. See the following value list. Perhaps you'll get lucky and find some in Aunt Minnie's cellar.

ITEM	DESCRIPTION & REMARKS	DOLLAR VALUE RANGES BY COLOR			
		Blue	Green	Pink	Yellow
Bowl	5" (cream soup)	—	—	42-53	—
Bowl	5½"	27-33	79-89	18-23	57-69
Bowl	7"	43-52	130-157	24-28	131-163
Bowl	9" (console, 3-legged)		—	2160-2350	—
Bowl	9½" (oval)	45-57	117-144	24-28	114-145
Bowl	10"	55-63		19-23	131-165
Bowl	10" (covered)	110-123	—	72-87	258-363
Bowl	11¾"	60-70	26-33	45-58	114-149
Bowl	12" (scalloped edge)	66-76	32-38	45-58	131-161
Butter Dish and cover		250-300	950-1040	66-75	950-1040
Cake Plate 10" (footed)		53-69	84-95	26-30	—
Candy Dish and cover		156-188	450-555	48-58	348-498
Celery Dish 9" (sectioned)		—	132-159	—	130-180
Celery Dish 10" (plain or sectioned)		36-44	120-145	24-30	114-155
Cookie Jar and cover		162-189	540-650	39-49	540-650
Creamer		66-76	156-188	18-22	156-188
Cup		45-57	156-185	14-19	156-185
Decanter with stopper		—	—	114-139	—
Goblet	3¾"	—	410-460	444-502	—
Goblet	4", 2½ oz.	—	—	110-128	—
Goblet	4", 3½ oz.	—	308-350	72-88	—
Goblet	4½"	—	308-350	72-88	—
Goblet	5¼"	—	444-502	444-502	

MAYFAIR (OPEN ROSE)

ITEM	DESCRIPTION & REMARKS	DOLLAR VALUE RANGES BY COLOR			
Goblet	5¾"	—	310-352	58-64	—
Goblet	7¼"	120-140	—	122-150	—
Pitcher	6"	110-138	430-500	40-49	435-500
Pitcher	8"	120-145	400-445	45-57	400-445
Pitcher	8½"	156-188	430-500	72-88	430-500
Plate	6"	13-18	72-84	11-13	72-88
Plate	6½"	—	—	21-15	—
Plate	6½" (ringed off-center)	31-35	102-118	29-35	—
Plate	8½"	31-34	84-96	19-25	84-96
Plate	9½"	55-69	114-145	53-64	114-144
Plate	9½" (grill)	33-39	84-96	32-39	84-96
Plate	11½" (grill with handles)	—	—	—	114-144
Plate	12" (cake, handled)	57-70	32-40	35-41	—
Platter	12½" (oval with open or closed handles)	—	—	—	192-222
Relish	8 3/8" (plain or 4-sectioned)	44-55	156-190	26-30	138-168
Salt and Pepper	(pair)	194-226	640-750	53-69	640-750
Salt and Pepper	(footed)	—	—	2100-2360	—
Sandwich Server	(center handled)	59-75	29-35	36-42	132-164
Saucer	(ringed)	—	—	29-35	—
Saucer		—	—	12-15	—
Sherbet	2¼"	78-93	—	92-110	—
Sherbet	3" (footed)	—	—	15-18	—
Sherbet	4¾" (footed)	57-71	160-200	72-87	72-82
Sugar		57-70	160-200	23-28	72-82
Sugar Cover		—	850-990	700-780	850-990
Tumbler	3½"	102-122	—	32-43	—
Tumbler	4¼"	90-108	—	32-38	—
Tumbler	4¾"	110-126	192-238	84-95	—
Tumbler	5¼"	102-120	—	39-51	—
Tumbler	3¼" (footed)	—	—	72-87	—
Tumbler	5¼" (footed)	102-120	—	36-42	192-232
Tumbler	6½" (footed)	114-145	230-280	39-51	—
Vase		84-95	190-230	110-133	—
Whiskey Jigger 2¼", 1½ oz.		—	—	90-101	—

MISS AMERICA
1933 - 1937

Hocking Glass Company

(now Anchor-Hocking Glass Corporation)

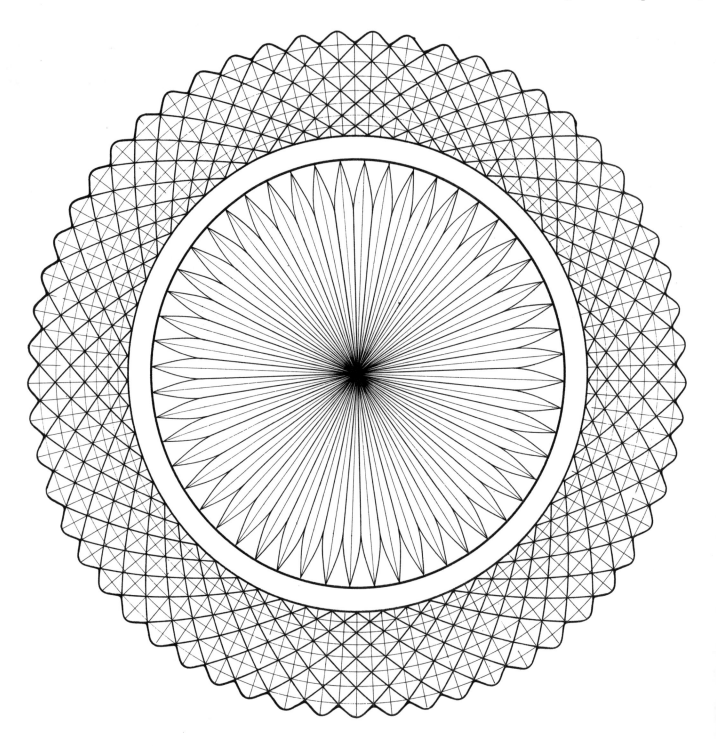

Colors found to date:

- Blue
- Crystal
- Green
- Pink
- Red

MISS AMERICA

Reproductions or Reissues

Covered buttered dishes and salt and pepper shakers have been reproduced in Miss America in crystal, blue, green, pink and amber. A physical comparison is the best way to tell the difference between old and new but if that is not practical, the cover presents the best evidence. If you invert the cover and feel inside just beneath the knob and can discern a definite round protrusion, you have an original. The new covers don't exhibit this rounded protrusion. Also, if you hold the old one up to a light and look from inside, outward through the knob, you will see a distinct geometrical star. If you look at the new cover the same way, the star is there but it is uneven with indistinct points.

The reproduction salt and pepper shakers are crude, hobs don't have the sharp feel of the original and the lower portion next to the square base seems filled with glass. The inside depth of the old is about one-half inch deeper than the reproduction. The colors of the reproductions are crystal, green and pink.

Pitchers and tumblers have been reproduced. The new tumblers have twice as thick bottoms as the originals. The handles on the old are just below a hump on the rim of the pitcher top. New ones have no hump.

General Pattern Notes

New collectors have a tendency to confuse "Miss America" with "English Hobnail". Turn back to page 65-66 and read the discussion of the differences.

Red is the color to look for in Miss America. Any piece in red is a real prize. Pink and crystal are the most commonly found and collected colors.

Of the rare pieces the butter dish and cover intact, as well as the shakers, 8-inch and 8½-inch pitchers, and pink goblets are all quite desirable.

ITEM	DESCRIPTION & REMARKS	DOLLAR VALUE RANGES BY COLOR			
		Crystal	Green	Pink	Red
Bowl	4½"	—	12-15	—	—
Bowl	6¼"	8-10	14-18	14-18	—
Bowl	8"	39-48	—	66-76	300-350
Bowl	8¾"	36-43	—	55-69	—
Bowl	10" (oval)	13-18	—	21-28	—
Butter Dish and cover		225-257	—	445-506	—
Cake Plate 12" (footed)		24-30	—	37-44	—
Candy Jar and cover 11½"		72-89	—	132-153	—
Celery Dish 10½"		12-15	—	21-26	—
Coaster 5¾"		21-24	—	29-35	—
Compote 5"		14-18	—	21-26	—
Creamer (footed)		11-13	—	17-19	144-170
Cup		12-14	13-15	21-25	—
Goblet 3¾"		24-28	—	66-76	162-207
Goblet 4¾"		26-32	—	66-76	162-207
Goblet 5½"		26-30	—	47-59	162-207
Pitcher 8"		78-93	—	122-150	—
Pitcher 8½"		92-102	—	132-152	—
Plate 5¾"		3-6	8-11	6-8	—
Plate 6¾"		—	11-13	—	—
Plate 8½"		6-9	13-15	15-21	90-101
Plate 10¼"		14-16	—	24-30	—
Plate 10¼" (grill)		11-13	—	15-20	—

ITEM	DESCRIPTION & REMARKS	DOLLAR VALUE RANGES BY COLOR			
Platter	12¼" (oval)	14-18	—	21-25	—
Relish	8¾" (4 sections)	11-13	—	18-23	—
Relish	11¾" (sectioned, round)	21-26	—	156-188	—
Salt and Pepper (pair)		32-38	324-374	60-71	—
Saucer		3-6	—	6-8	—
Sherbet		11-13	—	17-21	—
Sugar		10-11	—	16-19	134-159
Tumbler	4"	21-25	—	55-63	—
Tumbler	4½"	19-33	21-27	31-37	—
Tumbler	6¾"	32-38	—	66-76	—

DEPRESSION GLASS
Key For Cover Photos

GREEN	TOPAZ or YELLOW	ULTRAMARINE	AMBER (Light)
CREMAX	FOREST GREEN	PINK	FROSTED or PINK SATIN FINISH
PINK (Orange Cast)	MONAX	**COBALT**	GREEN OPALESCENT

FRONT COVER

BACK COVER

CRYSTAL	RUBY RED	CRYSTAL on METAL BASE	IRIDESCENT
JADITE	LIGHT BLUE	DELPHITE	AMETHYST
SHELL PINK	AMBER (Dark)	OPALESCENT	IRIDESCENT

MODERNTONE
1934 - late 1940's

Hazel Atlas Glass Company   Clarksburg, West Virginia and Zanesville, Ohio

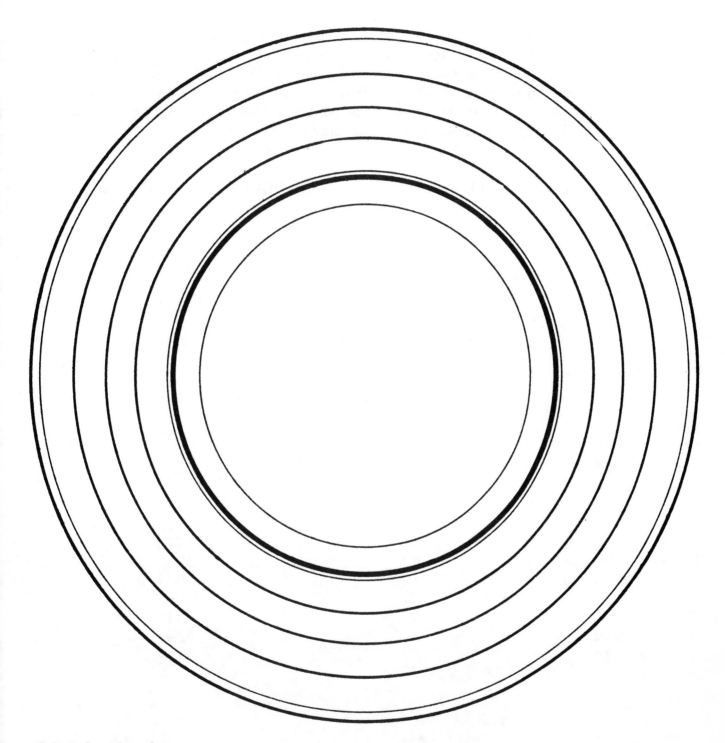

Colors found to date:

- Amethyst ("Burgundy")   • Blue (Cobalt)   • Crystal
- Pink   • *Platonite

*Platonite was a heat resistant opaque coating that was applied to the pieces and fired onto them like a glaze. There are at least eight different colors to be found.

MODERNTONE

Reproductions or Reissues
None known to date.

General Pattern Notes
Moderntone is also called "Wedding Band". A very simple but attractive design. Moderntone is found mostly in the cobalt blue. Very few pieces are found in pink or crystal. At present they are not particularly sought for it is believed that there weren't enough pieces made in those colors to warrant collecting them. Blue and amethyst 7½-inch bowls are practically impossible to find. The butter dish and cheese dishes, each with metal covers, and the ash trays would make a collector jump for joy if they were to pick them up as bargains at flea markets or yard sales.

ITEM	DESCRIPTION & REMARKS	DOLLAR VALUE RANGES BY COLOR	
		Amethyst	Blue (Cobalt)
Ash Tray		—	132-162
Bowl	4¾" (cream soup)	14-17	12-25
Bowl	5"	11-13	13-25
Bowl	5" (cream soup, ruffled edge)	17-19	21-26
Bowl	6½"	36-43	43-55
Bowl	7½"	36-43	44-55
Bowl	8¾"	24-30	29-35
Butter Dish and metal cover		—	90-105
Cheese Dish and metal cover, 7"		—	102-127
Creamer		8-10	8-11
Cup		6-8	7-10
Cup		13-16	13-16
Plate	5¾"	3-6	3-6
Plate	6¾"	5-7	5-7
Plate	7¾"	6-9	6-9
Plate	8 7/8"	11-14	11-14
Plate	10½"	15-23	15-23
Platter	11" (oval)	17-22	17-22
Platter	12" (oval)	30-35	36-42
Salt and Pepper (pair)		40-49	32-38
Saucer		3-6	3-6
Sherbet		6-10	6-10
Sugar and metal cover		32-44	32-44
Tumbler	9 oz.	—	15-18
Whiskey Jigger	1½ oz.	—	13-15

MOONSTONE

1941 - 1946

Anchor-Hocking Glass Corporation

Colors found to date:

- Crystal with white opalescent highlights
- Green with opalescent highlights

Reproductions or Reissues

None known to date.

General Pattern Notes

There is no pattern drawing with this listing for the pattern design is virtually the same as that of "Hobnail" on page 94-95. The difference is that the hobs and edges of the glass in Moonstone are opalescent. Moonstone also has some rough edge pieces.

Up until recently it was thought that the opalescent white was the only color manufactured, but it is now known that green was also produced. The green is quite rare and presently too unique to value.

ITEM	DESCRIPTION & REMARKS	DOLLAR VALUE RANGES BY COLOR
		Opalescent Hobnails
Bonbon	(heart shaped)	10-12
Bowl	5½"	10-12
Bowl	5½" (ruffled)	6-9
Bowl	6½" (handled)	10-12
Bowl	7¾"	11-14
Bowl	7¾" (relish, sectioned)	10-12
Bowl	9½"	14-17
Bowl	(cloverleaf shaped)	11-14
Candleholders (pair)		20-25
Candy Jar and cover, 6"		24-28
Cigarette Box and cover		18-24
Creamer		9-10
Cup		7-10
Goblet		20-24
Plate	6¼"	3-6
Plate	8"	10-12
Plate	10"	17-22
Powder Puff Box and cover, 4¾"		21-25
Saucer		3-6
Sherbet	(footed)	9-10
Sugar	(footed)	9-10
Vase, Bud		13-16

MT. PLEASANT or DOUBLE SHIELD

c. 1930

L. E. Smith Glass Company

MT. PLEASANT.
This drawing is the bottom
side of a black 6½" piece. The pattern
design does not appear on the upper surface.

*Colors found to date:

        • Black   • Blue   • Green   • Pink

*Amber was mentioned in early catalogs.

MT. PLEASANT
or
DOUBLE SHIELD

Reproductions or Reissues
None known to date.

General Pattern Notes
There seems to be quite a variety of shapes in this pattern. Some would not appear to belong at first glance but old catalogs illustrate them together as "Mt. Pleasant". There are round and square plates, the former with scalloped edges and the latter with scallops alternating with single and double points. Some pieces are found with gold handles and some with gold edge trim. There have been several black pieces found with sterling silver surface decorations. Most of these are worn off with heavy use and can be difficult to detect.

ITEM	DESCRIPTION & REMARKS	DOLLAR VALUE RANGES BY COLOR	
		Black or Blue	Green or Pink
Bowl	(3-legged)	26-30	18-24
Bowl	8" (scalloped, 2-handled)	24-30	17-19
Bowl	8" (square, 2-handled)	25-29	15-18
Candlesticks	(single stem, pair)	25-29	19-23
Candlesticks	(pair)	42-55	29-35
Creamer		18-24	13-15
Cup		10-12	6-8
Plate	8" (2 styles)	14-16	11-12
Plate	8" (closed handles)	18-24	12-14
Plate	10½" (closed handles)	29-34	21-26
Salt and Pepper	(pair)	36-43	25-29
Saucer	(2 styles)	3-6	3-6
Sherbet		14-17	8-10
Sugar		18-24	13-15

NEW CENTURY
C. 1930

Hazel Atlas Glass Company

Clarksburg, West Virginia and Zanesville Ohio

Flat pieces such as plates and the other items bear this alternating wide and narrow band pattern also and some of them exhibit radiated patterns out from two concentric circles or ovals as in lower illustration of a plate.

Colors found to date:

- Amethyst
- Crystal
- Black
- Green
- Blue (Cobalt)
- Pink

130

Reproductions or Reissues
None known to date.

General Pattern Notes
Green is the predominant color in this pattern. Only a very few pieces have been found in other colors, with crystal leading the list as having been uncovered in the most different pieces.

Ash trays and decanters are among the more scarce items in any color.

There have been reports of some fired-on opaque colors: red, blue, yellow and green.

ITEM	DESCRIPTION & REMARKS	DOLLAR VALUE RANGES BY COLOR	
		Amethyst, Cobalt or Pink	Crystal or Green
Ash Tray		—	35-45
Bowl	4½"	—	5-8
Bowl	4¾" (cream soup)	—	11-15
Bowl	8"	—	12-18
Bowl	9" (covered casserole)	—	66-76
Butter Dish and cover		—	66-76
Cup		12-15	5-9
Creamer		—	8-11
Decanter with stopper		—	52-63
Goblet	2½ oz.	—	15-17
Goblet	3¼ oz.	—	20-22
Pitcher	7¾" (2 styles)	27-37	31-41
Pitcher	8" (2 styles)	38-53	33-45
Plate	6"	—	3-7
Plate	7 1/8"	—	6-11
Plate	8½"	—	8-11
Plate	10"	—	12-19
Plate	10" (grill)	—	10-16
Platter	11" (oval)	—	12-19
Salt and Pepper (shakers, pair)		—	32-43
Saucer		5-8	3-7
Sherbet	3"	—	6-11
Sugar and cover		—	16-26
Tumbler	3½"	9-12	10-15
Tumbler	4 1/8"	9-12	10-15
Tumbler	5"	11-15	12-17
Tumbler	5¼"	14-17	17-24
Tumbler	4" (footed)	—	11-15
Tumbler	4 7/8" (footed)	—	13-19
Whiskey Jigger 2½"		—	7-11

NEWPORT

1936 - 1940

Hazel Atlas Glass Company

Clarksburg, West Virginia and Zanesville, Ohio

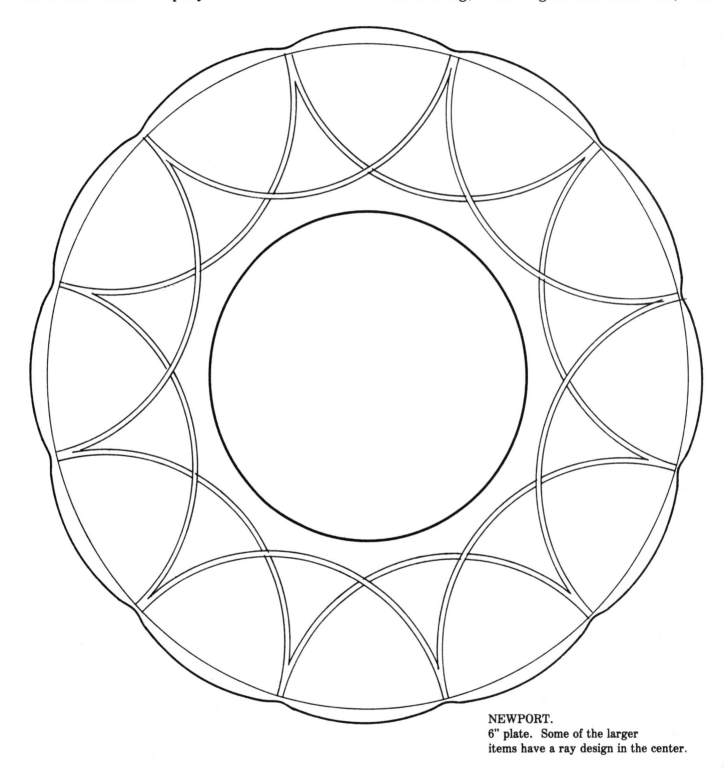

NEWPORT.
6" plate. Some of the larger
items have a ray design in the center.

Colors found to date:

- Amethyst ("Burgundy")
- Blue (Cobalt)
- Platonite (various colors)
- Pink

NEWPORT

Reproductions or Reissues
    None known to date.

General Pattern Notes
    Value for amethyst, cobalt blue and a few pieces in pink are so nearly the same that the listing here lumps them together. The other colors would be valued at about one-half or a little more of the values listed.
    Newport is sometimes called "Hairpin."

ITEM	DESCRIPTION & REMARKS	DOLLAR VALUE RANGES BY COLOR	
		Cobalt Blue or Amethyst	Platonite (White)
Bowl	4¼"	6-9	3-6
Bowl	4¾" (cream soup)	13-17	9-12
Bowl	5¼"	14-17	9-12
Bowl	8¼"	19-23	12-14
Cup		6-9	3-6
Creamer		9-11	4-7
Plate	6"	3-6	2-5
Plate	8½"	8-11	4-9
Plate	11½"	21-28	12-15
Platter	11¾" (oval)	25-30	14-17
Salt and Pepper	(shakers, pair)	45-52	29-36
Saucer		3-6	2-5
Sherbet		10-12	6-8
Sugar		9-11	4-7
Tumbler	4½"	21-28	12-16

NORMANDIE

1933 - 1940

Federal Glass Company

Columbus, Ohio

Colors found to date:

- Amber
- Crystal
- Pink

NORMANDIE

Reproductions or Reissues
None known to date.

General Pattern Notes
There are some who call this pattern "Bouquet and Lattice".

Some iridescent items are showing up and they tend to bring a bit higher price than the other pieces in isolated cases.

The pattern was first produced in pink and crystal, followed by an iridescent amber, then a true clear amber.

The salt and pepper shakers, pitchers and covered sugars are the most sought-after items in this pattern.

ITEM	DESCRIPTION & REMARKS	DOLLAR VALUE RANGES BY COLOR		
		Amber	Iridescent	Pink
Bowl	5"	6-9	6-9	6-9
Bowl	6½"	10-13	10-13	10-13
Bowl	8½"	12-17	12-17	12-17
Bowl	10" (oval)	13-15	20-23	26-32
Creamer	(footed)	7-10	7-10	7-10
Cup		6-9	6-9	6-9
Pitcher	8"	54-64	—	97-114
Plate	6"	3-6	3-6	3-6
Plate	8"	9-11	30-35	9-11
Plate	9¼"	7-11	7-11	7-11
Plate	11"	20-24	20-24	38-52
Plate	11" (grill)	12-17	12-17	12-17
Platter	11¾"	12-17	12-17	20-24
Salt and Pepper	(shakers, pair)	42-54	—	60-70
Saucer		3-6	3-6	3-6
Sherbet		7-11	7-11	7-11
Sugar		6-10	6-10	6-10
Sugar Cover		90-102	—	126-143
Tumbler	4"	15-19	—	33-40
Tumbler	4¼"	13-17	—	26-32
Tumbler	5"	20-25	—	33-40

OLD CAFE

1936-1940

Hocking Glass Company   **Lancaster, Ohio**

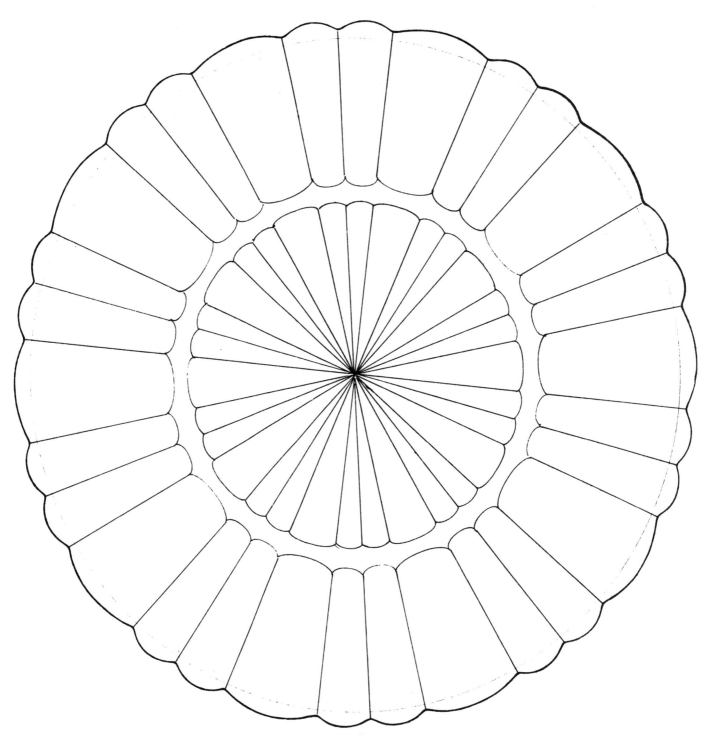

Colors found to date:

• **Crystal 1936-1938**   • **Pink 1936-1938**

• **Royal Ruby Red 1940**

OLD CAFE

Reproductions or Reissues
    None known to date.
General Pattern Notes
    In 1940 Hocking made a few assorted pieces in their Royal Ruby Red color. It is known that they sometimes mixed crystal and red in items such as cups and saucers and covered candy dishes. The pitchers are scarce in all colors.

ITEM	DESCRIPTION OR REMARKS	VALUE RANGES BY COLOR	
		Crystal and Pink	Royal Ruby
Bowl	3¾"	2-4	5-7
Bowl	5", one handled	2-5	—
Bowl	5", two handled	3-5	11-13
Bowl	5½"	5-7	11-13
Bowl	9", two handled, closed	10-13	15-18
Candy	8", covered	6-10	12-16
Cup		3-6	7-10
Pickle or Olive Dish 6", handled, oblong		5-8	—
Pitcher	6", 36 oz.	60-75	—
Pitcher	9", 80 oz.	87-113	—
Plate	6"	2-4	—
Plate	10"	16-22	—
Saucer		2-5	—
Sherbet	footed	5-8	—
Tumbler 3"		5-8	—
Tumbler 4"		5-9	—
Vase	7¼"	11-13	16-22

OYSTER AND PEARLS

1938 - 1940

Anchor-Hocking Glass Corporation

Colors found to date:

• Crystal   • Opaque White   • Pink   • Ruby Red

OYSTER AND PEARLS

Reproductions or Reissues
None known to date.

General Pattern Notes
Only a small number of items are available in this pattern. They are all accessory or serving pieces.

The opaque white pieces are white on the outside and pink or green on the inside.

ITEM	DESCRIPTION & REMARKS	DOLLAR VALUE RANGES BY COLOR		
		Crystal or Pink	Red	Opaque white with fired-on Green or Pink
Bowl	5¼"	5-8	12-14	7-10
Bowl	5¼" (heart shape)	5-9	—	7-10
Bowl	6½" (handled)	11-14	15-19	—
Bowl	10½"	20-24	40-49	15-17
Candleholder 3½" (pair)		20-24	42-51	20-23
Plate	13½"	12-14	36-44	—
Relish Dish 10¼" (2 sections)		5-9	—	10-12

PARROT

1931 - 1932

Federal Glass Company   Columbus, Ohio

Colors found to date:

- Amber
- Blue*
- Crystal
- Green

*Only one piece known at present, but lends evidence that there might be more.

PARROT

Reproductions or Reissues
None known to date.

General Pattern Notes
Parrot is also known sometimes as "Sylvan". Sylvan was the name given the pattern by the company, but it is much better known and identified by the name "Parrot".

The pattern was in production for only a very short period of time.

Green is the color found most often followed by amber. The other colors are in short supply.

ITEM	DESCRIPTION & REMARKS	DOLLAR VALUE RANGES BY COLOR	
		Amber	Green
Bowl	5"	15-22	15-22
Bowl	7"	39-47	31-39
Bowl	8"	86-104	78-93
Bowl	10" (oval)	60-75	33-76
Butter Dish and cover		685-865	315-380
Creamer	(footed)	31-40	29-34
Cup		31-40	28-34
Hot Plate	5"	—	360-420
Pitcher	8½"	—	685-865
Plate	5¾"	15-21	15-21
Plate	7½"	—	21-27
Plate	9"	29-35	31-39
Plate	10½" (grill, round)	—	23-29
Plate	10½" (grill, square)	23-27	—
Plate	10¼" (square)	36-44	36-44
Platter	11¼"	66-79	36-44
Salt and Pepper (shakers, pair)		—	190-235
Saucer		13-16	13-16
Sherbet	(footed)	20-27	20-27
Sherbet	4¼"	—	170-215
Sugar		24-32	24-32
Sugar Cover		165-210	78-93
Tumbler	4¼"	86-104	86-104
Tumbler	5½"	110-143	113-135
Tumbler	5¾" (footed)	120-170	113-136

PATRICIAN
1933 - 1937

Federal Glass Company   Columbus, Ohio

Colors found to date:

• Amber   • Crystal   • Green   • Pink

Reproductions or Reissues
None known to date.

General Pattern Notes
The company named this pattern "Spoke" but it is more popularly known as "Patrician".

Amber is the more commonly collected color because there is more of it available. There are, however, shortages in some amber pieces due to its popularity.

Covered pieces, pitchers and tumblers in any color are the most desirable; therefore values are high relative to the rest of the collection.

ITEM	DESCRIPTION & REMARKS	DOLLAR VALUE RANGES BY COLOR		
		Amber or Crystal	Green	Pink
Bowl	4¾" (cream soup)	14-18	25-30	24-29
Bowl	5"	11-13	11-13	14-18
Bowl	6"	23-27	21-25	21-26
Bowl	8½"	36-43	26-31	26-27
Bowl	10" (oval)	25-30	15-21	17-20
Butter Dish and cover		95-111	120-145	255-315
Cookie Jar and cover		79-88	240-295	—
Creamer	(footed)	11-12	11-12	12-15
Cup		11-13	11-13	11-13
Pitcher	8"	96-111	114-149	155-188
Pitcher	8¼"	137-158	114-149	155-188
Plate	6"	11-13	6-8	4-7
Plate	7½"	13-15	13-15	21-25
Plate	9"	11-13	9-11	9-11
Plate	10½"	6-9	26-29	21-26
Plate	10½" (grill)	12-14	14-19	14-18
Platter	11½" (oval)	14-18	22-26	17-21
Salt and Pepper	(pair)	55-67	66-77	113-131
Saucer		6-8	6-8	6-8
Sherbet		11-13	14-18	14-18
Sugar		8-10	11-13	11-13
Sugar Cover		39-45	60-70	60-70
Tumbler	4"	28-33	28-33	28-33
Tumbler	4½"	25-30	23-28	24-28
Tumbler	5½"	36-43	39-46	48-57
Tumbler	5¼" (footed)	44-53	60-70	—

PEACOCK AND ROSE (No. 300)

1928 - 1930's

Paden City Glass Manufacturing Company   Paden City, West Virginia

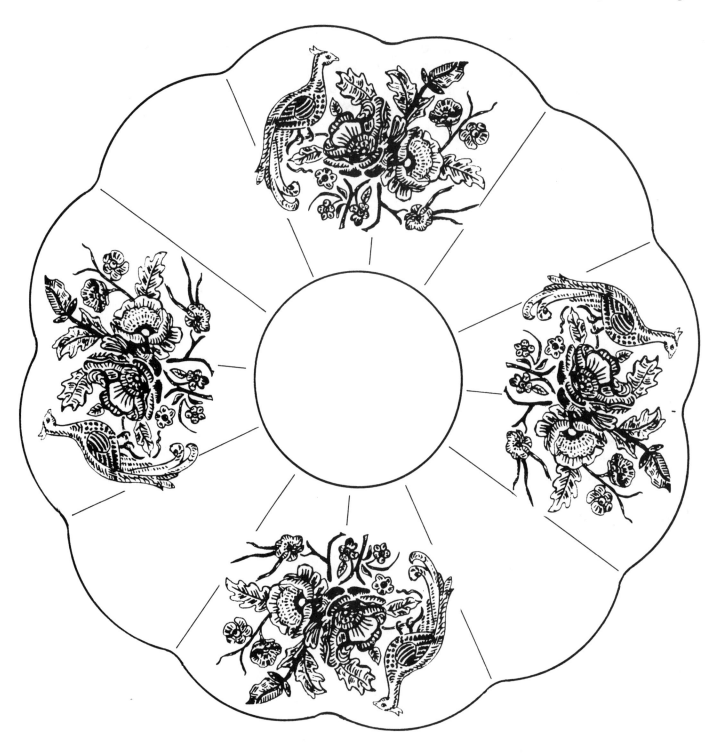

Colors found to date:

- Blue (Cobalt)   • Green   • Pink

PEACOCK AND ROSE (No. 300)

Reproductions or Reissues
    None known to date.

General Pattern Notes
    Paden City's number 300 line consists of many items. The blanks were utilized widely by the company for etching all sorts of designs.
    The Peacock and Rose design is very hard to find, with the cups being the rarest.

ITEM	DESCRIPTION & REMARKS	DOLLAR VALUE RANGES BY COLOR
		Green or Pink
Bowl	8½"	33-40
Bolw	8½" (oval, footed)	44-54
Bowl	8¾" (footed)	33-40
Bowl	9¼" (footed)	36-43
Bowl	9¼" (center handle)	41-50
Bowl	10½"	42-52
Bowl	10½" (footed)	42-53
Bowl	10½" (center handle)	41-50
Bowl	11" (console, rolled edges)	41-50
Bowl	14" (console, rolled edges)	51-60
Cake Plate		42-52
Candlesticks (pair)		38-50
Candy Dish and cover (footed)		71-84
Compote	6¼"	29-36
Creamer	4½" (footed)	30-36
Cup		77-89
Ice Bucket	5¾"	64-74
Mayonnaise Set (3 pieces)		53-65
Plate	8"	19-24
Plate	10½"	26-32
Relish	(3 sections, covered)	26-32
Saucer		24-27
Sugar	4¼"	30-36
Vase	10"	66-80

PEANUT BUTTER
1950's

Manufacturer Unknown

Colors found to date:

  • Crystal, tumblers and sherbets in milk glass

Reproductions & Reissues
 None known to date

General Pattern Notes
 Very little is known about this pattern other than the fact that the water glass was the container in which Big Top Peanut Butter was sold in the early to mid 1950's. Only five other pieces have turned up so far. It has been reported that the water glass and sherbet have shown up in milk glass. This is as yet unsubstantiated. Crystal is the color you will find the pattern in.

DESCRIPTION & REMARKS		DOLLAR VALUE RANGE BY COLOR
		Crystal
Plate	8"	3-6
Cup		2-4
Saucer		2-4
Sherbet	(footed)	2-5
Juice Glass	5¼"	8-10
Water Glass	5¾"	3-6

DEPRESSION GLASS
Key For Cover Photos

GREEN	TOPAZ or YELLOW	ULTRAMARINE	AMBER (Light)
CREMAX	FOREST GREEN	PINK	FROSTED or PINK SATIN FINISH
PINK (Orange Cast)	MONAX	COBALT	GREEN OPALESCENT

FRONT COVER

BACK COVER

CRYSTAL	RUBY RED	CRYSTAL on METAL BASE	IRIDESCENT
JADITE	LIGHT BLUE	DELPHITE	AMETHYST
SHELL PINK	AMBER (Dark)	OPALESCENT	IRIDESCENT

PETALWARE

1930 - 1940

Macbeth-Evans Glass Company   Charleroi, Pennsylvania

Colors found to date:

- Cobalt Blue
- Monax
- Cremax
- Pink
- Crystal
- Various fired on colors

PETALWARE

Reproductions or Reissues
  None known to date.

General Pattern Notes
  In 1930 Macbeth-Evans released Petalware in pink and crystal. In the following years they added many variations of the cremax and monax by painting different colorful designs on them.
  Only *four pieces are known to exist presently in the cobalt blue. Those are the 8¾ inch bowl, the footed creamer, footed sherbet and footed sugar bowl. All are worth in excess of $30.00
  The value listing below is for all colors and designs.

*There is a fifth piece in cobalt, the metal cover mustard, but it is fairly common and valued at only about $7.00 to $8.00.

ITEM	DESCRIPTION & REMARKS	DOLLAR VALUE RANGES BY COLOR
		All colors
Bowl	4½" (cream soup)	5-13
Bowl	5¾"	4-11
Bowl	7"	9-12
Bowl	8¾"	5-14
Cup		3-8
Creamer		3-10
Lamp Shade	(2 sizes)	7-16
Mustard with metal cover		5-9
Pitcher		24-30
Plate	6"	2-6
Plate	8"	2-8
Plate	9"	4-8
Plate	11"	5-12
Plate	12"	9-17
Platter	13" (oval)	9-17
Saucer		2-6
Sherbet	4" (footed)	13-17
Sherbet	4½" (footed)	4-10
Sugar	(footed)	3-9
Tidbit Servers		15-27
Tumblers		3-11

PINEAPPLE AND FLORAL (No. 618)

1932 - 1937

Indiana Glass Company

Dunkirk, Indiana

Colors found to date:

- Amber
- Crystal
- Green
- Red (fired-on color)
- White

PINEAPPLE AND FLORAL (No. 618)

Reproductions or Reissues
There were some pieces reissued in the 1970's in an avocado green and milk white.

General Pattern Notes
The amber and fired-on red color are the more valuable pieces in this pattern. Although there are no extraordinary high value items in the pattern, the tumblers and most of the bowls are becoming hard to find.

ITEM	DESCRIPTION & REMARKS	DOLLAR VALUE RANGES BY COLOR	
		Amber or Red	Crystal
Ash Tray		26-32	21-26
Bowl	4¾"	21-25	27-33
Bowl	6"	24-29	24-27
Bowl	7"	14-18	8-10
Bowl	(cream soup)	29-34	25-29
Bowl	10" (oval)	23-29	23-29
Compote	(diamond shape)	11-13	2-5
Creamer	(diamond shape)	14-18	11-13
Cup		11-13	11-12
Plate	6"	5-7	3-6
Plate	8 3/8"	8-10	6-9
Plate	9½"	15-20	14-16
Plate	11½"	18-23	17-20
Platter	11" (closed handles)	15-19	13-15
Platter	11½" (relish, sectioned)	14-16	23-28
Saucer		3-6	3-6
Sherbet	(footed)	18-23	18-23
Sugar	(diamond shaped)	14-16	11-13
Tumbler	4¼"	36-46	33-39
Tumbler	4½"	31-38	31-38
Vase	(cone shape, with metal holder)	—	32-38

PRETZEL
1930's-1970's

Indiana Glass Company

Dunkirk, Indiana

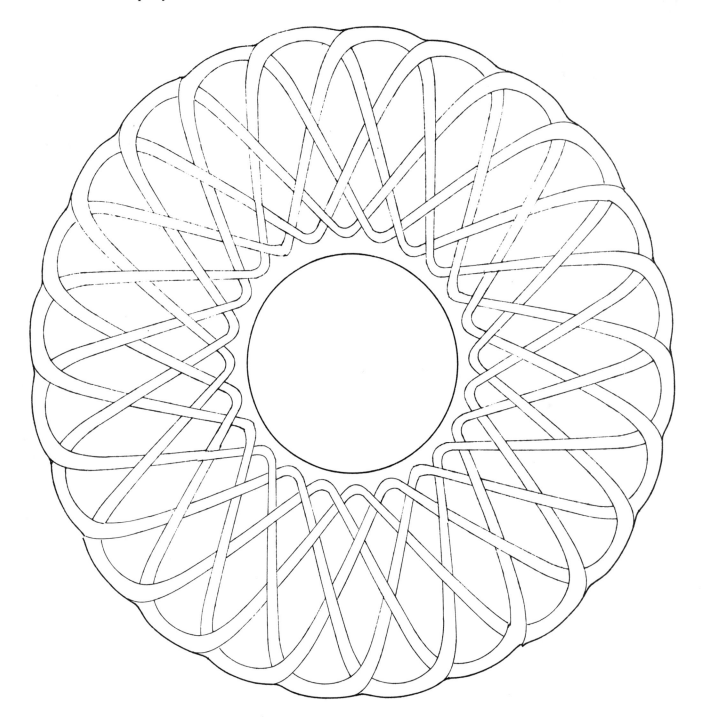

Reproductions or Reissues

The two handled pickle dish, leaf shaped olive dish and the celery dish have all been made in quantity into the 1970's.

General Pattern Notes

The company catalogs identified this pattern only as No. 622, but collectors have dubbed it "Pretzel" for obvious reasons. It is an inexpensive pattern to collect, but has a limited number of pieces in the line. A pitcher and three sizes of tumblers may be found. They are listed in catalogs, but it is not known that any have ever turned up. The company may never have produced them.

DESCRIPTION & REMARKS		DOLLAR RANGE BY COLOR
		Crystal
Bowl	7½"	4-7
Bowl	9⅜"	10-11
Celery Dish	10¼"	4-5
Creamer		6-7
Sugar		4-7
Cup		4-7
Saucer		1-3
Olive Dish	(leaf shaped), 7"	1-4
Pickle Dish	(2-handled), 8½"	2-5
Pickle Dish	(tab handled)	2-5
Plate	6"	1-3
Plate	8⅜"	2-5
Plate	9⅜"	5-7
Plate	11½"	8-10
Sherbet		5-6

PRINCESS
1931 - 1935

Hocking Glass Company   (now Anchor-Hocking Glass Corporation)

Colors found to date:

- Amber (Topaz or Dark Yellow)   • *Blue   • Green
  • Pink   • Yellow

*Suspected to be a reproduction from Mexico. This is not substantiated.

Reproductions or Reissues

    Suspected. See footnote.

General Pattern Notes

    First to be produced in 1931 was the green and then came the dark yellow color (amber or topaz), but the darker yellow was soon discontinued.

    Rarest of the items in this pattern are the pitchers (footed), a six-inch yellow pitcher, and yellow covered butter dishes.

    Hocking also used a frosted finish on some of their Princess items.

    There is no true saucer for cups in this pattern. They are the same as the five and one-half inch sherbet plates.

ITEM	DESCRIPTION & REMARKS or Amber	DOLLAR VALUE RANGES BY COLOR		
		Green	Pink	Yellow
Ash Tray		71-86	88-102	105-120
Bowl	4½"	22-27	13-16	33-40
Bowl	5"	24-28	13-17	33-39
Bowl	9" (octagonal)	29-36	24-27	93-116
Bowl	9½" (hat shape)	30-36	21-25	108-122
Bowl	10" (oval)	18-22	14-18	51-62
Butter Dish and cover		93-109	85-117	455-520
Cake Stand 10"		20-23	15-18	—
Candy Dish and cover		44-52	50-58	—
Coaster		26-32	77-87	93-115
Cookie Jar and cover		39-53	55-65	—
Creamer	(oval)	11-14	13-15	13-16
Cup		11-13	5-9	9-10
Pitcher	6"	41-50	29-36	412-462
Pitcher	7 3/8" (footed)	460-515	368-423	—
Pitcher	8"	50-58	42-52	88-102
Plate	5½" (used as saucer)	4-7	3-6	4-7
Plate	8"	11-13	8-10	10-12
Plate	9½"	24-28	12-14	13-16
Plate	9½" (grill)	13-15	7-10	10-12
Plate	11½" (grill,closed handle)	10-12	5-9	10-12
Plate	11½" (handled)	13-15	11-14	13-16
Platter	12" (closed handles)	13-18	13-18	38-49
Relish	7½" (sectioned)	24-28	16-22	66-80
Relish	7½" (no sections)	70-86		132-157
Salt and Pepper 4½" (pair)		50-58	37-44	71-86
Spice Shakers 5½" (pair)		29-36	—	—
Sherbet	(footed)	20-24	13-18	33-40
Sugar and cover		24-30	23-27	26-32
Tumbler	3"	24-27	20-23	24-27
Tumbler	4"	26-32	15-18	24-27
Tumbler	5¼"	33-40	22-27	30-36
Tumbler	4¾" (footed)	66-80	55-65	—
Tumbler	5¼" (footed)	27-32	22-27	24-28
Tumbler	6½" (footed)	60-70	36-45	75-87
Vase	8"	30-36	24-28	—

PYRAMID (No. 610)

c. 1930

Indiana Glass Company

Dunkirk, Indiana

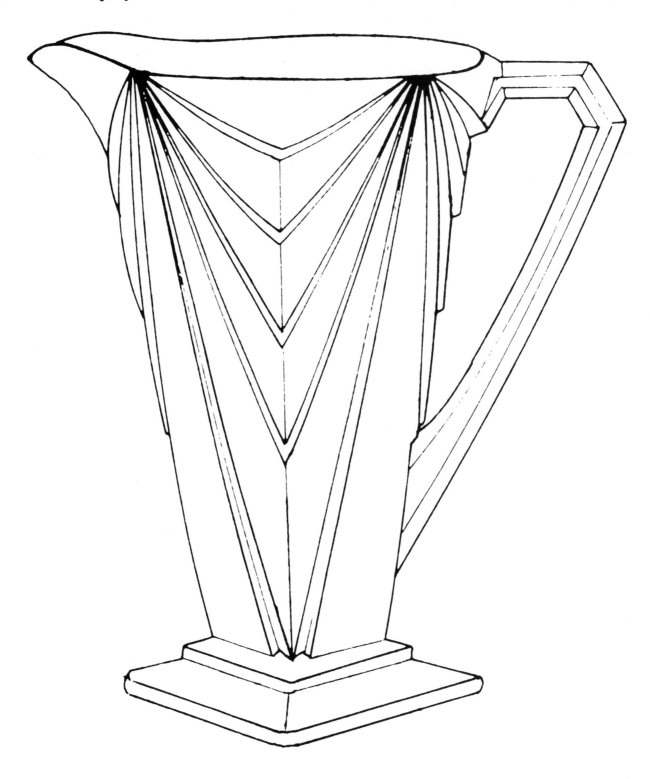

Colors found to date:

- Black
- Pink
- Crystal
- White (Opaque)
- Green
- Yellow

Reproductions or Reissues

Pyramid has been reissued twice. In the 1950's it was reissued in opaque white and topaz. In 1974 they began producing the pattern in black for distribution through Tiara Home Products. They were distributed exclusively through Tiara at home party sales.

General Pattern Notes

This pattern was apparently produced only in accessory tableware for there are no cups, dinner plates, etc.; primarily serving pieces.

There seems to be a dire shortage of any items in crystal, so be on the lookout for them. They should bring a premium price.

ITEM	DESCRIPTION & REMARKS	DOLLAR VALUE RANGES BY COLOR		
		Pink	Green	Yellow
Bowl	4¾"	14-17	16-19	26-32
Bowl	8½"	22-27	26-30	52-61
Bowl	9½" (oval)	28-32	26-32	55-65
Bowl	9½"	28-32	26-32	55-65
Creamer		22-27	22-28	26-32
Ice Tub		82-89	88-103	175-210
Ice Tub and cover		—	—	395-445
Pitcher		135-155	155-175	215-260
Relish Tray (handled, 4 sections)		27-34	27-34	60-70
Sugar		22-27	23-27	26-32
Tray for Creamer and Sugar		20-22	22-26	25-30
Tumbler	8 oz. (footed)	22-25	26-32	46-58
Tumbler	11 oz. (footed)	42-50	53-65	66-78

QUEEN MARY

1936 - 1940's

Hocking Glass Company

(now Anchor-Hocking Glass Corporation)

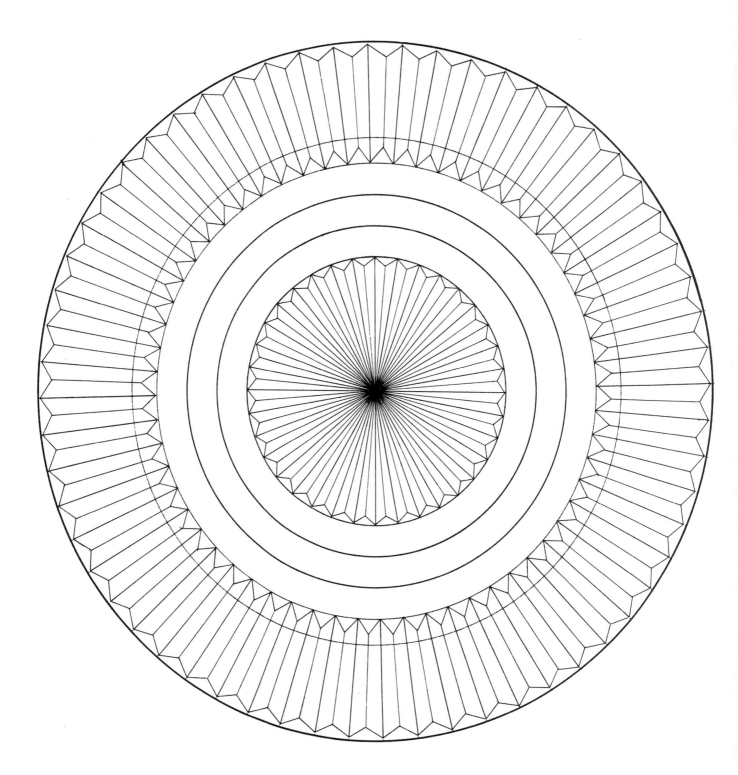

Colors found to date:

- Crystal
- *Green
- Pink
- Red (Ruby)

*Ash tray only. Made in the 1950's.

Reproductions or Reissues
None known to date.

General Pattern Notes
Sometimes called "Vertical Ribbed", Queen Mary was first produced in pink then came crystal. The ruby red was the latest, being released in the 1940's.

There are two distinct types of cups to be found.

The butter dish with cover, candy dish with cover, 9¾-inch plate and salt and pepper shakers when found in **pink** are worth anywhere from two to five times the values listed below.

ITEM	DESCRIPTION & REMARKS	DOLLAR VALUE RANGES BY COLOR
		Crystal or Pink
Ash Tray	2" x 3¾" (oval)	3-6
Bowl	4" (1 handle or no handle)	5-7
Bowl	5"	5-7
Bowl	5½" (2-handled)	5-7
Bowl	6"	5-7
Bowl	7"	6-9
Bowl	8¾"	11-13
Butter Dish and cover		36-42
Candy Dish and cover		31-38
Candlesticks 4½" (pair)		15-20
Candlesticks (red)		45-55
Celery Dish 5" x 10"		5-7
Cigarette Box (oval)		6-9
Coaster	3½"	3-6
Coaster	4¼" (square)	6-9
Compote	5¾"	6-9
Creamer	(oval)	6-8
Cup	(2 styles)	6-9
Plate	6"	3-6
Plate	6 5/8"	5-7
Plate	8½"	11-13
Plate	9¾"	11-13
Plate	12"	10-11
Plate	14"	12-15
*Punch Bowl Set (6 cups, bowl, metal rim for bowl, and ladle)		95-125
Relish Tray 12" (3 sections)		14-17
Relish Tray 14" (4 sections)		14-18
Salt and Pepper (shakers, pair)		22-26
Saucer		2-5
Sherbet	(footed)	5-7
Sugar	(oval)	6-9
Tumbler	3½"	3-6
Tumbler	4"	6-8
Tumbler	5" (footed)	21-26

*It is not likely that the metal rim and ladle will be found but, if so, what a lucky find!

RADIANCE

1935-1940

New Martinsville Glass Company

Colors Found To Date

- Amber
- Cobalt
- Crystal
- Ice Blue
- Red

Reproductions & Reissues
None known to date

General Pattern Notes
You will note in the value range listing below that the crystal items are lower than the others. If they are found with silver or gold rims or decorations they will command the same prices as the others. Cobalt is the rarest color.

DESCRIPTION & REMARKS		Crystal	Red	Amber & Ice Blue
Bowl	(2-handled), 5"	6-7	12-14	8-10
Bowl	6"	6-7	12-13	8-10
Bowl	(footed), 6"	7-8	14-16	10-12
Bowl	(covered), 6"	14-17	30-35	19-23
Bowl	(2-section relish), 7"	7-9	15-18	7-9
Bowl	(3-section relish)	10-12	21-26	12-14
Bowl	7"	7-8	14-16	12-14
Bowl	(ruffled edge), 10"	14-16	27-32	17-19
Bowl	(ruffled edge), 12"	17-19	33-37	21-24
Bowl	(flared edge), 10"	13-16	26-31	19-21
Bowl	(flared edge), 12"	17-19	33-37	21-24
Butter Dish		175-185	342-357	347-357
Candle Holder 8"		25-36	45-55	45-55
Candle Holder, (2-branch)		46-55	72-76	73-76
Celery Dish 10"		10-12	19-21	12-14
Cheese & Cracker Set, 11"		17-19	33-42	19-24
Compote	5"	6-7	12-14	7-9
Compote	6"	7-8	15-19	8-10
Condiment Set (4 pieces)		60-75	132-162	113-135
Creamer		7-8	14-16	11-13
Sugar		6-8	14-17	8-10
Cruet	(individual size)	18-21	36-41	30-35
Cup		4-7	11-13	8-10
Saucer		2-4	3-5	3-5
Decanter & Stopper		48-58	100-110	60-70
Lamp	12"	42-47	90-105	48-53
Mayonnaise Set (3 pieces)		18-20	36-40	21-24
*Pitcher	64 ounces	90-105	195-215	132-152
Plate	8"	3-5	8-10	6-8
Plate	14" (punch bowl base)	18-21	38-44	24-29
Punch Bowl		42-47	90-95	42-47
Punch Bowl Ladle		42-47	90-95	48-53
Punch Cup		3-5	7-9	3-6
Salt & Pepper		18-21	38-44	30-35
Tray	(oval)	12-14	24-29	18-23
**Tumbler 9 oz.		8-10	17-20	12-15
Vase	10"	19-23	42-47	30-35
Vase	12"	30-35	60-70	43-47

*Cobalt: 318-338
**Cobalt: 36-41

RAINDROPS

1927 - 1933
See "THUMBPRINT"

Federal Glass Company   Columbus, Ohio

Colors found to date:

• Crystal   • Green

Reproductions or Reissues
None known to date.

General Pattern Notes
"Raindrops" was first produced in 1927 in green tumblers only. Then came the rest of the line by 1929.

This pattern is frequently confused with another similar pattern by Federal, "Thumbprint", further confused here because there was no handy example piece of "Raindrops" to do a pattern drawing. If you will refer to the drawing of "Thumbprint" on page 202 it will become clear what the major difference is. In that drawing, notice that the impressions are more or less **pear-shaped**. It is not clear in the drawing, but the pear-shaped impressions of Thumbprint are actually **depressions** in the glass. In Raindrops pieces the designs are **round** and are **bumps**, not depressions. Once you have handled both you won't have any more trouble identifying them.

Covered sugars are the rarest of this pattern along with a **pair** of salt and peppers. For some unknown reason there is a shortage of pepper shakers.

Crystal pieces are seldom seen.

ITEM	DESCRIPTION & REMARKS	DOLLAR VALUE RANGES BY COLOR
		Green
Bowl	4½"	3-6
Bowl	6"	4-7
Cup		4-7
Creamer		8-11
Plate	6"	2-5
Plate	8"	3-6
Salt and Pepper	(shakers, pair)	72-86
Saucer		2-5
Sherbet		6-9
Sugar		6-9
Sugar Cover		36-44
Tumbler	3"	4-7
Whiskey Jigger	1 7/8"	4-8

RIBBON
1930 - 1931

Hazel Atlas Glass Company

Clarksburg, West Virginia and Zanesville, Ohio

Colors found to date:

- Black
- *Crystal
- Green
- *Pink

*Few examples have been found so far.

Reproductions or Reissues
None known to date

General Pattern Notes
The preponderance of color in this pattern is green. There are some black pieces but they are not highly sought but by a few collectors.

A very short-lived pattern, Ribbon may become quite popular owing to its fairly low prices. Remember what demand does to supply and prices.

As is the case so much of the time it's hard to find the covers for several pieces; therefore the covered candy dish in Ribbon commands the highest price in the pattern.

ITEM	DESCRIPTION & REMARKS	DOLLAR VALUE RANGES BY COLOR	
		Black	Green
Bowl	4"	—	3-6
Bowl	8"	26-44	19-25
Candy Dish and cover		—	33-40
Creamer	(footed)	14-18	6-8
Cup		—	4-7
Plate	6¼"	—	2-5
Plate	8"	14-16	3-6
Salt and Pepper (shakers, pair)		38-47	17-21
Saucer		—	2-5
Sherbet	(footed)	—	3-6
Sugar	(footed)	29-35	3-6
Tumbler	5½"	—	14-16
Tumbler	6½"	—	19-23

ROSE CAMEO
c. 1930

*Belmont Tumbler Company

Bellaire, Ohio

ROSE CAMEO. Border design detail. Turn to CAMEO by Hocking and note the very close similarity of the design so that you may learn how to keep from confusing them. The major difference is that ROSE CAMEO here has a rose within the cameo and CAMEO has a dancing girl in the cameo.

Colors found to date:

• Green only

Reproductions or Reissues
None known to date.

General Pattern Notes
Little is known about this pattern or its manufacturer at present. There is a patent of the design dated December 1, 1931 and granted to a Howard A. Lay.

Rose Cameo is sometimes confused with Hocking's "Cameo". All the collector has to do is note that there is no ballerina in the "Rose Cameo" design, to prevent the confusion.

So far no cups and saucers have been found.

*Unsubstantiated

ITEM	DESCRIPTION & REMARKS	DOLLAR VALUE RANGES BY COLOR
		Green
Bowl	4½"	4-7
Bowl	5"	6-9
Bowl	6"	12-14
Bowl	7"	6-8
Plate	7"	6-8
Sherbet		4-8
Tumbler	5" (footed)	12-14

ROSEMARY
1935 - 1937

Federal Glass Company

Columbus, Ohio

ROSEMARY or DUTCH ROSE. Basic pattern border design. This is the design found on cups. Larger pieces use the same design but the arch over the roses is raised so as to be continuous with the arches on either side. Arrows in drawing indicate position.

Colors found to date:

- Amber
- Crystal
- Green
- Pink

Reproductions or Reissues
None known to date.

General Pattern Notes
This is the final design that Federal settled upon after the "Mayfair" pattern was discontinued due to patent problems and the molds redesigned (see page 117-118).

Amber is the color most easily found but the most popular colors are the green and pink.

Rosemary is a simple attractive pattern, almost formal. It makes a very nice collection that is fairly inexpensive to put together.

ITEM	DESCRIPTION & REMARKS	DOLLAR VALUE RANGES BY COLOR	
		Amber	Green or Pink
Bowl	5"	3-6	6-8
Bowl	5" (cream soup)	10-14	18-23
Bowl	6"	7-10	17-19
Bowl	10" (oval)	10-12	19-23
Creamer	(footed)	8-9	12-14
Cup		4-7	6-9
Plate	6¾"	3-6	4-8
Plate		4-8	12-16
Plate	(grill)	4-8	8-12
Platter	12" (oval)	10-12	17-23
Saucer		2-5	3-6
Sugar	(footed, no handle)	8-11	10-14
Tumbler	4¼"	12-14	17-21

ROULETTE

1936 - 1937

Hocking Glass Company   (now Anchor-Hocking Glass Corporation)

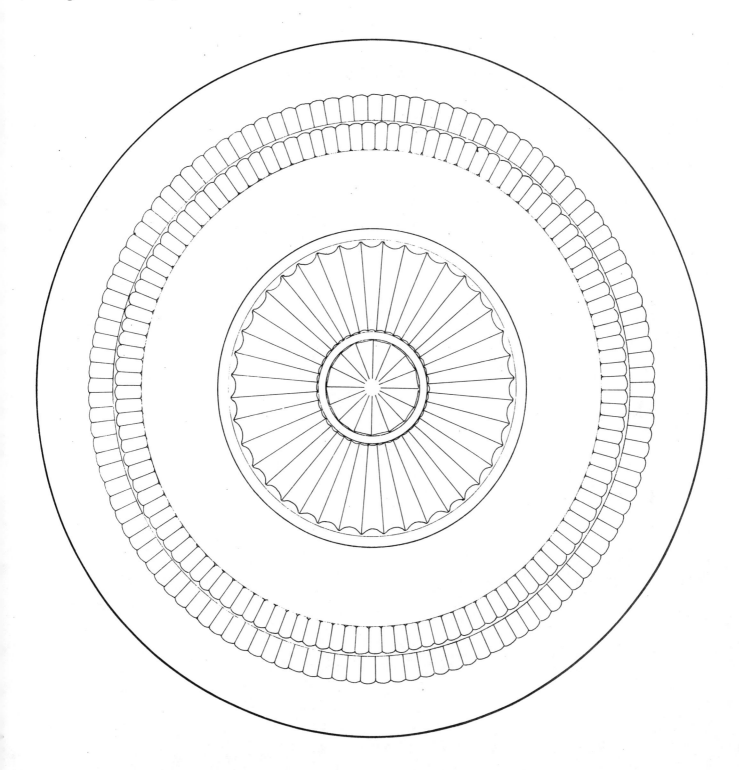

Colors found to date:

• Crystal   • Green   • Pink

ROULETTE

Reproductions or Reissues
None known to date.

General Pattern Notes
Another simple, plain design that comes off almost elegant.

It was made in crystal throughout production with some pink and green added. Prices for all of the colors are very close. Crystal may bring slightly more in some areas.

ITEM	DESCRIPTION & REMARKS	DOLLAR VALUE RANGES BY COLOR
		All colors
Bowl	9"	12-16
Cup		4-8
Pitcher	8"	29-35
Plate	6"	3-6
Plate	8½"	4-8
Plate	12"	12-14
Saucer		3-6
Sherbet		6-8
Tumbler	3¼", 5 oz.	6-8
Tumbler	3¼" (Old Fashion)	6-9
Tumbler	4 1/8"	14-18
Tumbler	5 1/8"	14-20
Tumbler	5½" (footed)	14-17
Whiskey Jiggers		10-14

ROUND ROBIN

C. 1930
Manufacturer unknown

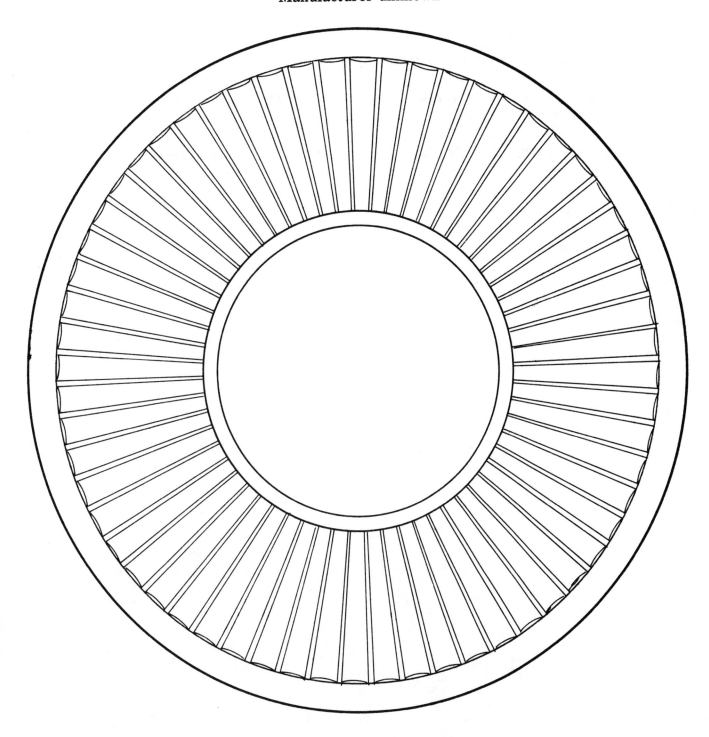

Colors found to date:

• Green   • Iridescent Amber

Reproductions or Reissues
None known to date.

General Pattern Notes
The Domino tray in the value listing was apparently made to hold the creamer and surround it with cubes of sugar as made by Domino.

Little is known about the origin of this pattern. Values for both colors are much the same, therefore they are lumped together as one.

ITEM	DESCRIPTION & REMARKS	DOLLAR VALUE RANGES BY COLORS
		All Colors
Bowl	4"	5-7
Cup	(footed)	5-7
Creamer	(footed)	6-9
Domino Tray	(round)	24-30
Plate	6"	2-5
Plate	8"	3-6
Plate	12"	5-7
Saucer		3-5
Sherbet		5-6
Sugar	(footed)	5-9

ROXANA

c. 1930

*Hazel Atlas Glass Company

Clarksburg, West Virginia and Zanesville, Ohio

Colors found to date: • Yellow

*Strongly suspected to be the manufacturer of this pattern.

ROXANA

Reproductions or Reissues
None known to date.

General Pattern Notes
So far only about six types of pieces have surfaced in this pattern. Little else is known.

ITEM	DESCRIPTION & REMARKS	DOLLAR VALUE RANGES BY COLOR
		Yellow
Bowl	4"	7-9
Bowl	5"	5-7
Bowl	6"	8-9
Plate	6"	4-6
Saucer		4-6
Sherbet	(footed)	5-7
Tumbler	4"	9-12

ROYAL LACE

1934 - 1941

Hazel Atlas Glass Company

Clarksburg, West Virginia and Zanesville, Ohio

Colors found to date:

- Amethyst (Burgundy)
- Crystal
- Green
- Blue (Dark)
- Pink

Reproductions or Reissues
None known to date.

General Pattern Notes
Pitchers are difficult to find. There were several design changes of pitchers over the years as well as the console bowls and candle holders. As usual, the covers for many items were broken or lost, making them more scarce and costly than their corresponding bowls.

The amethyst pieces are quite rare and command premium prices over the other colors.

Popularity of the other colors waxes and wanes frequently. This is a highly popular pattern with collectors, and the color preference changes with the whims of the collectors.

ITEM	DESCRIPTION & REMARKS	DOLLAR VALUE RANGES BY COLOR			
		Blue	Crystal	Green	Pink
Bowl	4¾"	30-35	12-15	36-44	14-19
Bowl	5"	31-37	11-13	26-29	17-20
Bowl	10" (round)	39-50	17-20	29-38	18-23
Bowl	10" (straight edge, 3 legs)	54-63	21-25	44-53	24-29
Bowl	10" (rolled edge, 3 legs)	190-225	116-140	98-108	26-30
Bowl	10" (ruffled edge, 3 legs)	69-79	29-35	55-69	26-30
Bowl	11" (oval)	42-52	21-25	30-37	24-29
Butter Dish and cover		430-480	78-93	290-350	144-169
Candlesticks		114-127	29-35	60-70	36-44
Candlesticks (rolled edge)		144-164	58-70	69-75	45-56
Candlesticks (ruffled edge)		105-125	32-38	69-83	48-70
Cookie Jar and cover		—	39-45	84-96	56-65
Cream	(footed)	12-15	14-17	26-32	33-40
Cup		30-37	7-10	26-30	11-13
Hot Toddy or Cider Set; Cookie Jar, Metal Lid, Metal Tray, 8 Roly-Poly Glasses and Ladle		156-175	—	—	—
Pitcher	54 oz. (straight sides)	102-120	44-53	98-116	53-69
Pitcher	8", 68 oz.	132-162	60-72	120-145	55-71
Pitcher	8", 86 oz.	155-186	66-76	144-169	84-97
Pitcher	8½"	190-230	72-84	162-192	92-115
Plate	6"	13-15	3-7	10-11	4-8
Plate	8½"	32-38	4-8	14-17	10-12
Plate	10"	36-48	11-13	26-30	12-14
Plate	9 7/8" (grill)	30-37	10-12	20-24	13-16
Platter	13" (oval)	52-60	22-26	36-42	26-30
Salt and Pepper (shakers, pair)		210-250	53-69	130-160	53-69
Saucer		11-14	3-7	7-9	4-8
Sherbet	(footed)	32-38	8-11	24-31	12-15
Sherbet and detachable metal holder		30-35	4-8	—	4-8
Sugar		30-38	8-11	21-25	11-13
Sugar Cover		98-116	18-23	36-46	17-21
Tumbler	3½"	37-46	11-14	27-34	15-20
Tumbler	4 1/8"	37-44	12-15	24-32	14-20
Tumbler	4 7/8"	45-57	14-20	36-44	21-24
Tumbler	5 3/8"	55-63	19-25	32-44	26-31

ROYAL RUBY

1939-1967

Anchor-Hocking Glass Corporation

Lancaster, Pennsylvania

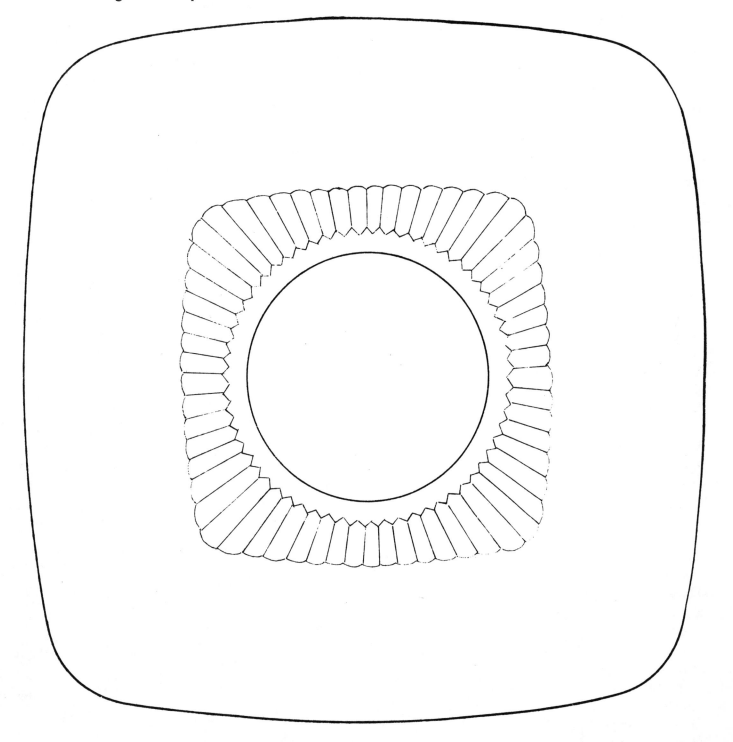

Colors found to date:

• Red only

ROYAL RUBY

Reproductions or Reissues

Tumblers, 9 oz., 10 oz. & 13 oz.; Ball Vase

Pattern Notes

Although Royal Ruby was meant originally by the company to describe color only, collectors use it as the name of this particular pattern. The company originally brought the pattern out in 1939-40. It is basically quite plain except for the vibrant red color. Later (1950s) they introduced the squared pieces such as plates and trays. These newer pieces usually contained a center ribbed design. At the same time they introduced the Roly-Poly type tumblers. You will sometimes find footed pieces with crystal bases.

ITEM	DESCRIPTION AND REMARKS	VALUE RANGES
Ash Tray	4½" square	3-5
Bowl	4¼"	3-6
Bowl	5¼"	7-9
Bowl	7½"	7-10
Bowl	8" oval	14-20
Bowl	8½"	14-20
Bowl	10" deep	18-23
Bowl	11½"	24-29
Creamer	plain	4-6
Sugar	plain	6-9
Creamer	footed	9-13
Sugar	footed, covered	18-23
Cup	round or squared	2-4
Goblet		7-14
Lamp		
Pitcher	22 oz., tilted	14-17
Pitcher	22 oz., upright	14-17
Pitcher	3 quart, tilted	24-28
Pitcher	3 quart, upright	24-28
Plate	6½"	2-4
Plate	7"	26-31
Plate	7¾"	3-9
Plate	9"	10-12
Plate	13¾"	14-20
Punch Bowl	with stand	24-29
Saucer	round or squared	1-3
Sherbet	footed	7-11
Tumbler	2½ oz., footed	9-13
Tumbler	3½ oz.	7-11
Tumbler	5 oz., 2 types	6-9
Tumbler	9 oz.	6-9
Tumbler	10 oz.	6-9
Tumbler	13 oz.,	9-14
Vase	ball type, 4"	3-5
Vase	6½"	3-6
Vase	assorted types and sizes	6-7

"S" PATTERN
1930 - 1933

Macbeth-Evans Glass Company

Charleroi, Pennsylvania

Colors found to date:

- *Amber
- Green
- Blue
- Pink
- *Crystal (with and without color bands)
- Red
- *Yellow

Reproductions or Reissues
None known to date.

General Pattern Notes
"S" Pattern is also known as "Stippled Rose Band". It is a busy but beautiful design. It is made particularly pretty to some collectors by the addition of bands of color in the rim-located stippled band design of the plates.

The three colors marked with an asterisk (*) in the preceding list are the colors most likely to be found. Any others have to be considered quite rare and the value is what you're willing to pay.

ITEM	DESCRIPTION & REMARKS	DOLLAR VALUE RANGES BY COLOR	
		Crystal	Amber, Yellow or Crystal (with color bands)
Bowl	5½"	3-7	4-8
Bowl	8½"	10-12	22-26
Creamer		6-9	9-11
Cup		3-7	4-8
Pitcher	80 oz.	48-64	110-120
Plate	6"	2-6	2-6
Plate	8"	3-7	3-8
Plate	9¼"	4-8	4-8
Plate	(grill)	3-7	4-8
Plate, cake	11"	45-59	45-57
Plate, cake	13"	78-103	78-101
Saucer		2-5	2-5
Sherbet	(footed)	4-8	5-9
Sugar		6-10	6-10
Tumbler	3½"	3-6	5-9
Tumbler	4"	4-7	6-10
Tumbler	4¼"	4-8	10-12
Tumbler	5"	6-8	10-12

SANDWICH

1939 - 1964

Hocking Glass Company

(now Anchor-Hocking Glass Corporation)

Colors found to date:

- Amber
- Pink
- Crystal
- Red (Ruby)
- Green (Dark)
- White (Opaque)

SANDWICH

Reproductions or Reissues

The company made their "Sandwich" pattern off and on throughout 25 years. Whether the collector wishes to call the later pieces reissues is up to individual discretion. They did reissue the cookie jar, but it is larger than the original and easily identified by examining it. They made no cover for this reissue in green. The others do have covers.

General Pattern Notes

Hocking first issued Sandwich in 1939-40, in green and ruby red, in a limited number of pieces, then sometime in the 1940's they released a full line of crystal. Sometime after the crystal came some pink and ruby red. Then in the 1950's they began producing more pieces in green and a small number of opaque white items. More green came in the late 1950's.

It is hard to determine whether Hocking produced all their colors continuously but considering the amount of each available one can surmise that most were.

Rarities in Hocking's Sandwich pattern include the small plate liner for the crystal custard; the pitchers, particularly the green ones; the butter dish and the cookie jar and cover; and bowls in green.

ITEM	DESCRIPTION & REMARKS	DOLLAR VALUE RANGES BY COLOR				
		Amber	Crystal	Green	Pink	Red
Bowl	4 7/8"	3-7	3-7	2-6	3-7	15-21
Bowl	5¼"	—	—	—	—	18-21
Bowl	6"	8-12	18-22	—	—	—
Bowl	6½"	10-12	7-9	31-40	—	—
Bowl	7"	—	10-13	43-54	—	—
Bowl	8"	—	8-11	48-56	13-17	44-55
Bowl	8¼" (oval)	—	—	—	—	—
Butter Dish		—	48-63	—	—	—
Cookie Jar and cover		50-64	43-53	26-29	—	—
Creamer		—	7-9	25-32	—	—
Cup		6-8	2-6	21-26	—	—
Custard Cup		—	3-7	2-6	—	—
Custard Cup liner		—	12-14	2-6	—	—
Pitcher	6"	—	58-78	126-171	—	—
Pitcher	2 quarts	—	72-87	228-278	—	—
Plate	7"	—	3-7	8-11	—	—
Plate	8"	—	3-7	—	—	—
Plate	9"	7-8	15-18	48-58	—	—
Plate	9" (ring for punch cup)	—	3-7	—	—	—
Plate	12"	13-17	12-13	—	—	—
Punch Bowl and stand		—	43-53	—	—	—
Punch Cups		—	3-7	—	—	—
Saucer		6-8	2-6	7-10	—	—
Sherbet	(footed)	—	7-9	—	—	—
Sugar and cover		—	15-20	22-25	—	—
Tumbler	5 oz.	—	7-8	3-7	—	—
Tumbler	9 oz.	—	8-11	3-7	—	—
Tumbler	9 oz. (footed)	—	20-25	—	—	—

SANDWICH

1920's to present

Indiana Glass Company   Dunkirk, Indiana

Colors found to date:

- Crystal
  - Teal (Blue-Green)
- Green
- Pink
- Red

SANDWICH

Reproductions or Reissues

This is a real bucket of worms. As with Hocking's Sandwich pattern, Indiana has been issuing various items and colors periodically over the years. The problem with this is that the company is **still** producing their Sandwich today. This is even further complicated by their production of several items for exclusive distribution through Tiara home party sales.

General Pattern Notes

The listing of values below is useful for all the colors, but use the values for crystal with caution. The market is very unstable to the down side presently and the values reflect that, but they can vary quite widely with dealers.

There are few reliable ways to distinguish old from new in Indiana's Sandwich pattern. The problem is that this applies to only two or three items. For instance, if you pick up a cup, a creamer of a sugar bowl and see the 1933 World's Fair inscription, then you **know**.

ITEM	DESCRIPTION & REMARKS	Crystal	Green or Pink	Red	Teal (Blue)
Ash Tray Set	(clubs, spades, hearts, diamonds)	13-16	22-26	—	—
Bowl	4¼"	3-5	4-7	—	—
Bowl	6"	3-5	4-7	—	—
Bowl	6" (6-sided)	4-7	—	—	9-11
Bowl	8¼"	11-13	13-17	—	—
Bowl	9" (console)	16-20	21-26	—	—
Bowl	10" (console)	22-25	25-31	—	—
Butter Dish and cover		38-55	160-190	—	215-248
Candlesticks	3½" (pair)	27-33	18-22	—	—
Candlesticks	7" (pair)	33-40	47-60	—	—
Creamer		9-11	9-11	38-48	—
Cruet and stopper		27-33	—	—	135-163
Cup		3-6	6-8	27-33	6-8
Creamer and Sugar	(on diamond-shaped tray)	16-22	—	—	33-46
Decanter and stopper		55-76	92-113	—	—
Goblet	9 oz.	16-22	18-24	—	—
Pitcher		44-70	96-130	—	—
Plate	6"	2-5	3-6	—	6-8
Plate	7"	3-6	4-7	—	—
Plate	8" (ringed off-center for sherbet)	5-8	7-9	—	10-14
Plate	8 3/8"	4-7	6-8	—	—
Plate	10½"	11-13	18-21	—	—
Plate	13"	11-13	18-22	—	—
Sandwich Service	(center handled)	16-22	37-48	—	—
Saucer		2-5	3-6	9-10	4-7
Sherbet		4-6	7-9	—	9-10
Sugar	(no cover)	9-11	12-14	35-48	—
Tumbler	3 oz. (footed)	17-22	20-26	—	—
Tumbler	8 oz. (footed)	13-17	17-21	—	—
Tumbler	12 oz. (footed)	22-28	30-37	—	—
Wine	3"	22-28	25-30	—	—

SHARON
1931 - 1933

Federal Glass Company

Columbus, Ohio

Colors found to date:

- Amber   • Crystal   • Green   • Pink

SHARON

Reproductions or Reissues

There have been reproductions of six items found in the Sharon pattern: shakers, covered butter, cheese dishes, candy dishes, sugars and creamers.

The salt and pepper shakers are poorly made as is the case of most of the reproductions. The pattern is the same but the leaves and flowers are not rendered very well. The roses don't look like roses as in the original.

In the genuine pattern covers for butter and cheese dishes are identical. So it is with the reproductions. The same problems exhibited on the shaker reproductions apply to the covers; however, the knob on top is the chief giveaway on the reproduction. On the reproduction the knob is easily grasped while on the old original the knob is flatter and there is little space between the bottom of the knob and the top of the cover, making it hard to grasp. So if you can pick up the top easily, beware.

The butter and cheese dishes themselves are thicker than the originals and have an overall awkward look. The ridge upon which the cover sits is more sharply defined and higher on the reproduction than on the original.

The colors the reproductions have been found in so far: blue, dark and light green, a color somewhat like topaz but reddish-brown, and pink.

General Pattern Notes

"Sharon" has been called "Cabbage Rose" in the past.

Although you will see crystal in the color list, there is too little of it around to be able to price it with any authority, so it doesn't appear in the value list below. Don't make the mistake of thinking crystal more valuable because of this. Crystal in fact is considerably less. A good guideline would be to price it at about one-fourth the values listed for amber pieces.

Rarities are the covered cheese, covered butter dish, the salt and pepper shaker pair and green, footed six and one-half inch tumblers.

ITEM	DESCRIPTION & REMARKS	DOLLAR VALUE RANGES BY COLOR		
		Amber	Green	Pink
Bowl	5"	7-11	11-14	11-13
Bowl	5" (cream soup)	22-26	39-52	39-52
Bowl	6"	14-18	21-26	21-26
Bowl	7½"	37-46	—	37-46
Bowl	8½"	5-8	25-32	17-21
Bowl	9½" (oval)	14-17	22-30	21-26
Bowl	10½"	24-31	31-38	24-32
Butter Dish and cover		57-73	110-125	60-75
Cake Plate	11½" (footed)	24-30	66-81	33-41
Candy Jar and cover		39-53	148-188	57-67
Cheese Dish and cover		181-206	—	600-720
Creamer	(footed)	11-14	17-24	14-19
Cup		12-16	14-18	14-19
Jam Dish	7½"	38-47	49-60	93-118
Pitcher	80 oz. (ice lip)	121-151	330-355	143-178
Pitcher	80 oz.	126-151	363-413	132-157
Plate	6"	3-7	5-8	5-8
Plate	7½"	13-16	19-24	23-30

SHARON

ITEM	DESCRIPTION & REMARKS		DOLLAR VALUE RANGES BY COLOR	
Plate	9½"	13-17	16-20	16-20
Platter	12½" (oval)	14-17	25-31	20-24
Salt and Pepper (shakers, pair)		49-60	82-94	53-73
Saucer		5-8	6-9	6-9
Sherbet (footed)		12-15	30-36	14-17
Sugar and cover		33-41	53-65	39-53
Tumbler	4 1/8"	30-37	47-60	31-38
Tumbler	5¼" (thin walled)	38-45	72-91	47-58
Tumbler	5¼" (thick walled)	38-45	77-97	68-81
Tumbler	6½" (footed)	68-81	—	47-60

Key For Cover Photos

GREEN	TOPAZ or YELLOW	ULTRAMARINE	AMBER (Light)
CREMAX	FOREST GREEN	PINK	FROSTED or PINK SATIN FINISH
PINK (Orange Cast)	MONAX	**COBALT**	GREEN OPALESCENT

FRONT COVER

BACK COVER

CRYSTAL	RUBY RED	CRYSTAL on METAL BASE	IRIDESCENT
JADITE	LIGHT BLUE	DELPHITE	AMETHYST
SHELL PINK	AMBER (DARK)	OPALESCENT	IRIDESCENT

SIERRA

1931 - 1933

Jeannette Glass Company   Jeannette, Pennsylvania

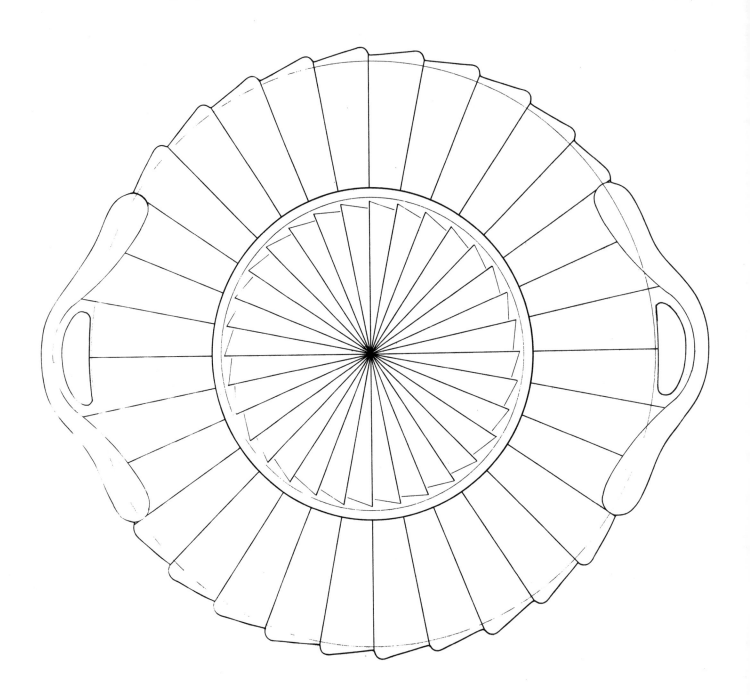

Colors found to date:

• Green   • Pink

SIERRA

Reproductions or Reissues
None known to date.

General Pattern Notes
Sierra was not in production long. Jeannette discontinued it because of the tendency of the points of the serrated edge to be easily broken. The pattern is moderately scarce because of the short production time. Sometimes known as "Pinwheel".

Pitchers, tumblers and covered butter dishes are among the items most difficult to obtain in Sierra. The combination Adam-Sierra design butter dish cover is coveted by collectors.

ITEM	DESCRIPTION & REMARKS	DOLLAR VALUE RANGES BY COLOR	
		Green	Pink
Bowl	5½"	10-13	10-12
Bowl	8½"	19-25	14-18
Bowl	9¼" (oval)	26-34	19-25
Butter Dish and cover		72-80	60-75
Creamer		15-20	14-18
Cup		14-16	11-13
Pitcher	6½"	102-107	54-61
Plate	9"	14-16	11-13
Platter	11" (oval)	21-29	18-23
Salt and Pepper (shaker, pair)		41-52	33-40
Saucer		5-8	6-7
Serving Tray (2-handled)		12-14	9-14
Sugar and cover		24-32	21-29
Tumbler	4½" (footed)	36-42	29-35

SPIRAL

Hocking Glass Company   1928 - 1930   (now Anchor-Hocking Glass Corporation)

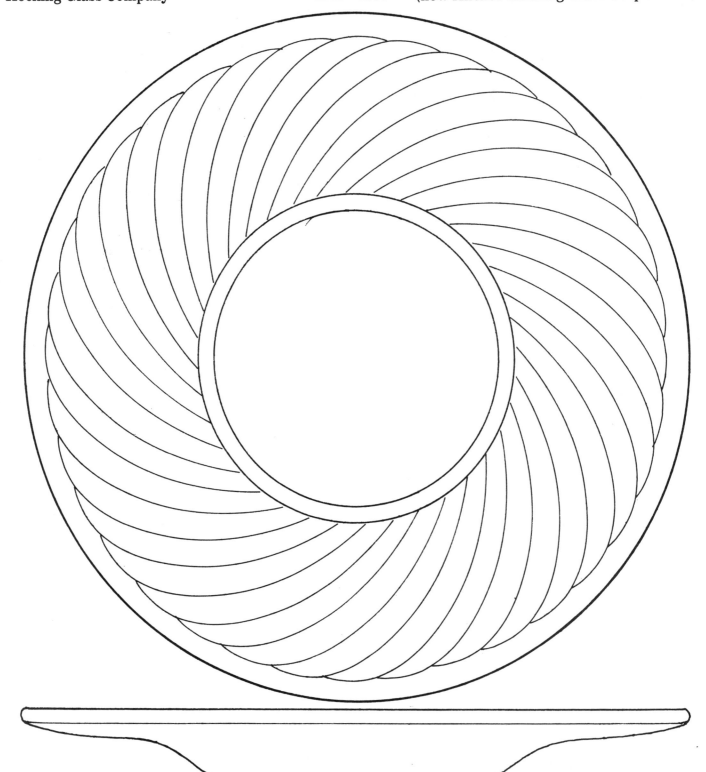

SPIRAL. One method collectors use to distinguish this pattern from the almost identical TWISTED OPTIC pattern is by the differing direction orientation of the spirals. As you can see the spirals are oriented in a clockwise direction here and those on the TWISTED OPTIC pieces are counterclockwise. This is so in the majority of the cases but not always. A more reliable way to tell the difference is to turn the plates over and examine the base. As you can see by the cross-section drawing here, the base flares out evenly from the bottom. If you will turn to the TWISTED OPTIC cross-section drawing you will be able to readily discern the difference.

SPIRAL

Colors found to date:

- *Crystal
- Green

Reproductions or Reissues
None known to date.

General Pattern Notes
Spiral is all to easily confused with Imperial's "Twisted Optic" pattern. The only reliable way to know the difference is to experience it. You should physically handle each if you have the opportunity. There are some unreliable methods based upon which way the spirals go, right or left.

An inexpensive way to get started in depression glass.

*Shown in an old catalog. It is not known if any is in collectors' hands.

ITEM	DESCRIPTION & REMARKS	DOLLAR VALUE RANGES BY COLOR Green
Bowl	4¾"	5-9
Bowl	7"	5-9
Bowl	8"	9-11
Creamer	(flat or footed)	5-9
Cup		4-8
Ice or Butter Tub		17-23
Pitcher	7 5/8"	24-32
Plate	6"	2-5
Plate	8"	3-7
Preserve and cover		22-32
Salt and Pepper	(shaker, pair)	22-32
Sandwich Server	(center handled)	22-28
Saucer		2-5
Sherbet		3-7
Sugar	(flat or footed)	5-8
Tumbler	3"	3-7
Tumbler	5"	4-8

STARLIGHT

1938 - 1940

Hazel Atlas Glass Company

Clarksburg, West Virginia and Zanesville, Ohio

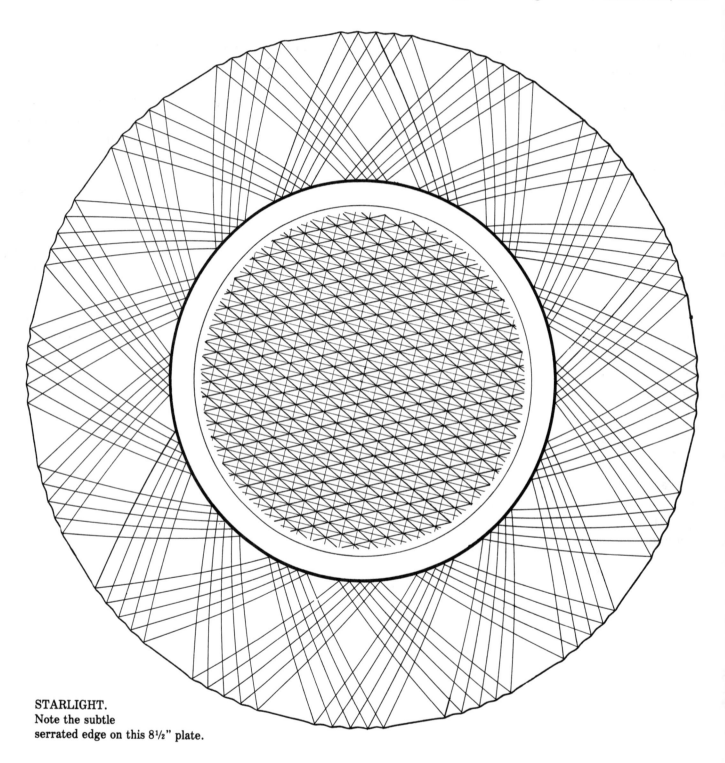

STARLIGHT.
Note the subtle
serrated edge on this 8½" plate.

Colors found to date:

- Blue (Cobalt)
- Crystal
- Pink
- White (Opaque)

STARLIGHT

Reproductions or Reissues
    None known to date.

General Pattern Notes
    The blue pieces seem to be available in limited numbers. The pattern is striking, but the values remain curiously low.

ITEM	DESCRIPTION & REMARKS	DOLLAR VALUE RANGES BY COLOR All Colors
Bowl	5½"	3-7
Bowl	4¾"	4-9
Bowl	8½" (closed handled)	6-13
*Bowl	11½" Salad	16-27
Plate	6"	3-7
Creamer	(oval)	4-8
Cup		3-7
Plate	8½"	3-7
Plate	9"	6-10
Plate	13"	6-13
Relish Dish		3-9
Salt and Pepper (shaker, pair)		17-22
Saucer		2-6
Sherbet		3-7
Sugar	(oval)	4-7

*There was a metal base designed for this bowl.

STRAWBERRY

c. 1930

U. S. Glass Company

Pittsburgh, Pennsylvania

Colors found to date:

- Crystal
- Green
- Pink

STRAWBERRY

Reproductions or Reissues
None known to date.

General Pattern Notes
"Strawberry" is occasionally found with the same pattern design but with cherries instead of strawberries. These pieces so far are the butter dish cover, the tumbler and pitcher. Pieces with the cherries are called "Cherryberry" by dealers and collectors. Their values generally run slightly higher than the regular pieces in pink or green.

Pitchers and covered butter dishes are the plums in this pattern. The butter dish covers have the same design motif, but the dishes themselves have only a center rayed design, no berries.

ITEM	DESCRIPTION & REMARKS	DOLLAR VALUE RANGES BY COLOR	
		Crystal or Iridescent	Green or Pink
Bowl	4"	6-9	10-12
Bowl	6¼"	30-36	49-59
Bowl	6½"	11-14	13-19
Bowl	7½"	13-18	20-24
Butter Dish and cover		143-175	167-204
Compote	5¾"	12-14	16-22
Creamer	(small)	12-14	14-18
Creamer	4 5/8"	15-18	21-27
Olive Dish	5" (1-handled)	11-13	13-15
Pickle Dish	8¼" (oval)	11-13	13-16
Pitcher	7¾"	179-204	148-176
Plate	6"	4-8	5-9
Plate	7½"	10-12	13-15
Sherbet		9-11	10-12
Sugar	(small, no cover)	14-18	20-24
Sugar	(large, covered)	32-38	42-52
Tumbler	3 5/8"	21-25	31-36

SUNFLOWER

c. 1930

Jeannette Glass Company   **Jeannette, Pennsylvania**

Colors found to date:

- *Delphite
- Green
- Pink

*Very rare. Insufficient data to establish realistic values at present.

SUNFLOWER

Reproductions or Reissues
    None known to date.

General Pattern Notes
    The rarest piece in the Sunflower pattern is the seven-inch trivet or hot plate. It has three legs and a raised edge.
    The cake plate is the most commonly found item.

ITEM	DESCRIPTION & REMARKS	DOLLAR VALUE RANGES BY COLOR
		Green or Pink
Ash Tray	5" (center design only)	12-14
Cake Plate	10" (3-legged)	12-14
Creamer	(Opaque: 72-87)	12-14
Cup		11-14
Hot Plate or Trivet	7"	150-180
Plate	9"	12-14
Saucer		3-7
Sugar	(Opaque: 72-87)	11-14
Tumbler	4¾" (footed)	19-25

SWIRL

1937 - 1938

Jeannette Glass Company

Jeannette, Pennsylvania

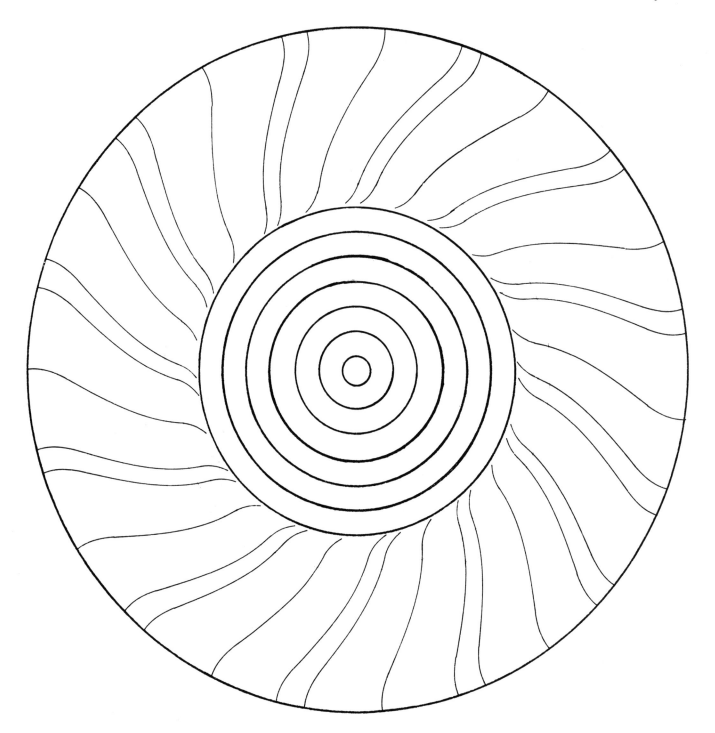

Colors found to date:

- Amber
  - Pink
- Blue
  - Aquamarine (Green-Blue)
- Delphite

Reproductions or Reissues
None known to date.

General Pattern Notes
"Swirl" has been referred to as "Petal Swirl" also.

Very little delphite was made and acquiring the covered butter dishes will be painful to the pocketbook, with the covered candy dish running into a sizeable outlay as well. Blue and amber anything would be a nice catch.

ITEM	DESCRIPTION & REMARKS	DOLLAR VALUE RANGES BY COLOR		
		Delphite	Pink	Ultramarine
Ash Tray		—	9-11	—
Bowl	5¼"	13-15	6-10	11-13
Bowl	9"	22-27	12-17	20-26
Bowl	10" (footed, with handles)	—	—	31-41
Bowl, Console	10½" (footed)	—	18-24	24-32
Butter Dish and cover		—	154-164	220-270
Candleholders	(double, pair)	—	86-94	33-39
Candleholders	(single, pair)	104-129	—	—
Candy Dish	(no cover, 3-legged)	—	6-10	11-15
Candy Dish with cover		—	72-83	88-108
Coaster		—	8-11	9-13
Creamer	(footed)	11-13	9-12	11-15
Cup		6-11	4-8	9-13
Pitcher	(footed)	—	—	705-790
Plate	6½"	4-8	3-7	4-8
Plate	7¼"	—	5-8	9-13
Plate	8"	5-8	5-8	12-16
Plate	9¼"	8-10	8-10	12-16
Plate	10½"	13-17	—	—
Plate	12½"	—	9-12	16-22
Platter	12" (oval)	27-35	—	—
Salt and Pepper	(shaker, pair)	—	—	31-39
Saucer		3-7	2-5	3-7
Sherbet	(footed)	—	8-11	12-15
Soup	(handled)	—	18-24	17-24
Sugar	(footed)	11-13	6-10	10-15
Tumbler	4"	—	10-13	14-19
Tumbler	4 5/8"	—	12-17	—
Tumbler	4¾"	—	20-24	33-43
Tumbler	9 oz. (footed)	—	15-19	24-32
Vase	6½" (footed)	—	13-17	21-28
Vase	8½" (footed)	—	—	23-29

TEA ROOM
1926 - 1931

Indiana Glass Company

Dunkirk, Indiana

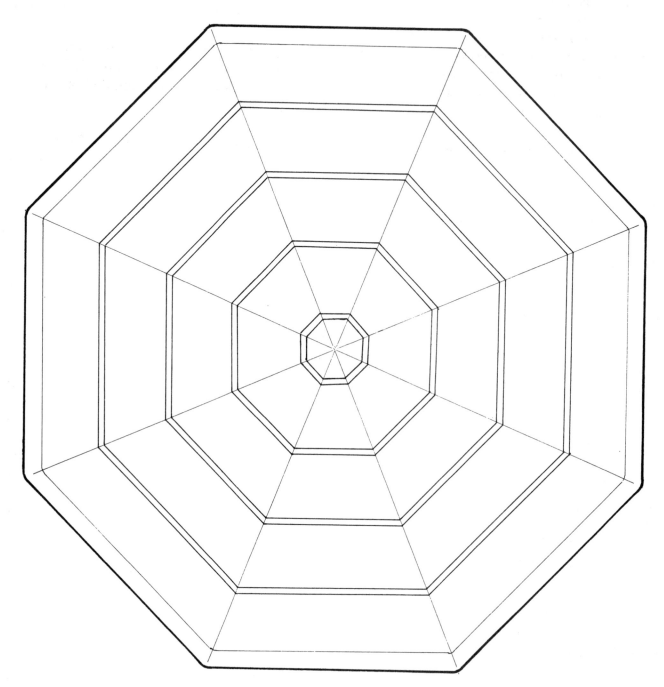

Colors found to date:

- Amber
- Crystal
- Green
- Pink

TEA ROOM

Reproductions or Reissues
    None known to date.

General Pattern Notes
    This pattern line is quite large and has a great variety of items in it. For instance, there are at least seven different sizes and styles of tumblers.
    In spite of the size of the line and its production being primarily for soda fountains and tea rooms, little of it seems to have survived the years. It is also difficult to locate mint items. It is heavy but angular and sharp edged in design, so it was subject to much chipping when handled or washed.
    Anything found in amber, and the pitcher in crystal, will bring a premium price.

ITEM	DESCRIPTION & REMARKS	DOLLAR VALUE RANGES BY COLOR Green or Pink
Bowl	7½" (banana split)	19-25
Bowl	8½"	21-29
Bowl	8¾"	53-61
Bowl	9½" (oval)	55-65
Candlestick	(pair)	41-53
Creamer	4"	15-20
Creamer	4½" (footed)	19-23
Creamer	(rectangular)	17-19
Creamer and Sugar with Tray, 3½"		54-69
Cup		24-29
Electric Lamp		42-57
Goblet		36-42
Ice Tub		43-55
Mustard with cover		66-86
Parfait		26-32
Pitcher		108-142
Plate	6½"	14-20
Plate	8¼"	26-34
Plate	10½" (2-handled)	31-39
Relish	(sectioned)	13-18
Salt and Pepper (shaker, pair)		50-60
Saucer		14-18
Sherbets	(3 styles)	17-22
Sugar	4"	13-18
Sugar	4½" (footed)	19-23
Sugar	(rectangular)	17-19
Sugar and cover		50-62
Sundae	(footed)	22-30
Tumbler	8½" oz.	24-32
Tumbler	6 oz. (footed)	19-23
Tumbler	9 oz. (footed)	19-23
Tumbler	11 oz. (footed)	24-29
Tumbler	12 oz. (footed)	33-44
Vase	6"	33-45
Vase	9"	36-46
Vase	11"	38-46

THISTLE

c. 1930

Macbeth-Evans Glass Company

Charleroi, Pennsylvania

Colors found to date:

- Crystal
- Green
- Pink
- *Yellow

*In very short supply. Not often found.

THISTLE

Reproductions or Reissues
   None known to date.

General Pattern Notes
   Pink is the more prevalent color available, but know that the pattern is fairly hard to find in any color.
   The large pink bowl is the prize in this pattern, but the pitcher and cake plate are both highly desirable in any color.

ITEM	DESCRIPTION & REMARKS	DOLLAR VALUE RANGES BY COLOR	
		Green	Pink
Bowl	5½"	20-26	13-17
Bowl	10¼"	110-135	148-168
Cup		20-28	17-24
Plate	8"	13-17	11-13
Plate	10¼" (grill)	15-21	15-21
Plate, Cake	13"	93-104	93-104
Saucer		11-14	11-14

THUMBPRINT

1927 - 1930

Federal Glass Company

Columbus, Ohio

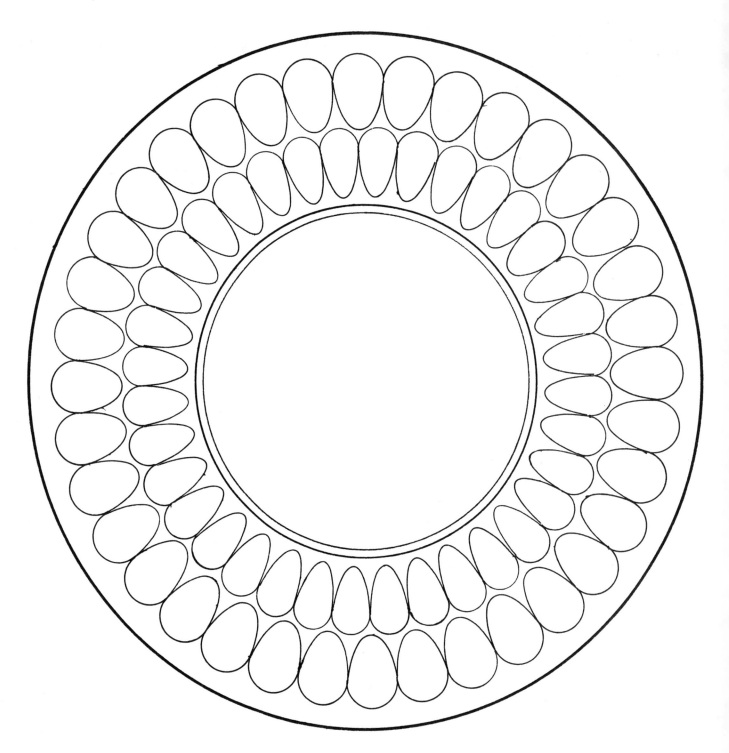

Colors found to date: • Green only

THUMBPRINT

Reproductions or Reissues
    None known to date.

General Pattern Notes
    This pattern was made primarily for promotional giveaways in cups and saucers.
    "Thumbprint" is easily confused with their similar "Raindrops" pattern. Please turn back to page 162 for an explanation of the differences.
    The sugar bowl and creamer are scarce.

ITEM	DESCRIPTION & REMARKS	DOLLAR VALUE RANGES BY COLOR Green
Bowl	4¾"	3-5
Bowl	5"	3-5
Bowl	8"	7-9
Creamer	(footed)	5-8
Cup		3-6
Plate	6"	2-5
Plate	8"	3-5
Plate	9¼"	4-7
Salt and Pepper	(shaker, pair)	18-26
Saucer		2-4
Sherbet		5-7
Sugar	(footed)	5-8
Tumbler	4"	4-6
Tumbler	5"	4-7
Tumbler	5½"	5-8
Wiskey Jigger 2¼"		4-7

TWISTED OPTIC
1927 - 1930

Imperial Glass Company

Bellaire, Ohio

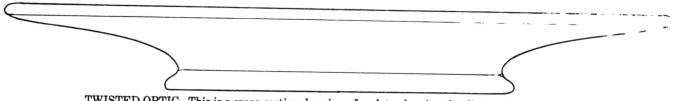

TWISTED OPTIC. This is a cross-section drawing of a plate showing the distinctive shape of the base in TWISTED OPTIC plates. The overall pattern design is identical to that of SPIRAL except for this base and that the majority of TWISTED OPTIC items have a counter clockwise spiraling. The SPIRAL pattern items are oriented in a clockwise direction. This latter observation is not always so making it a bit unreliable as a positive identification characteristic.

Colors found to date:

- Amber
- *Blue
- Green
- Pink
- *Yellow

Reproductions or Reissues
None known to date.

General Pattern Notes
Be careful not to confuse this pattern with Hocking's "Spiral". Please refer back to "Spiral" for discussion of how to tell the difference.

*Matched sherbets and ringed plates have been found but they are presently too unique to assign a realistic value.

ITEM	DESCRIPTION & REMARKS	DOLLAR VALUE RANGES BY COLOR
		All colors
Bowl	4¾"	6-10
Bowl	5"	3-6
Bowl	7"	6-10
Bowl, Console	10½"	16-22
Bowl, Console	11½"	18-24
Candlesticks	3" (pair)	12-16
Candy Jar and cover		18-26
Candy Jar and cover	(footed)	20-26
Creamer		5-8
Cup		3-6
Pitcher		20-24
Plate	6"	2-4
Plate	7"	3-5
Plate	7½" x 9" (oval)	4-7
Plate	8"	3-5
Powder Box with cover		16-22
Preserve	(same as Candy Jar but with a slot in lid for server)	22-30
Sandwich Server	(center handled)	16-23
Sandwich Server	(2-handled)	7-9
Saucer		1-3
Sherbet		5-8
Sugar		5-8
Tumbler	4½"	5-8
Tumbler	5¼"	8-12

VERNON (No. 616)

1930 - 1933

Indiana Glass Company　　　　　　　　　　　　　Dunkirk, Indiana

Colors found to date:

- Crystal　　　　• Green　　　　• Yellow

VERNON (No. 616)

Reproductions or Reissues

None known to date.

General Pattern Notes

This is a very difficult pattern of depression glass to find. There are few pieces to be collected when you do find it.

The crystal pieces are becoming scarce, but the green still commands the higher prices.

ITEM	DESCRIPTION & REMARKS	DOLLAR VALUE RANGES BY COLOR		
		Crystal	Green	Yellow
Bowl	4½"	3-6	5-7	4-6
Bowl	6½"	4-7	4-8	4-7
Bowl	7½"	6-9	7-10	8-10
Bowl	9"	8-11	11-16	11-16
Creamer	(footed)	12-18	25-32	22-30
Cup		7-10	17-23	16-18
Pitcher	8½"	32-42	50-70	48-68
Plate	8"	7-9	8-12	9-14
Plate	11"	16-22	25-35	23-30
Plate	(grill)	6-9	8-12	8-12
Saucer		3-6	5-8	5-8
Sugar	(footed)	12-18	24-33	22-28
Tumbler	(small, footed)	12-16	25-33	23-28
Tumbler	(medium, footed)	16-20	27-34	26-32
Tumbler	(large, footed)	17-24	30-36	30-36

VICTORY
1929 - 1930's

Diamond Glass-Ware Company   Indiana, Pennsylvania

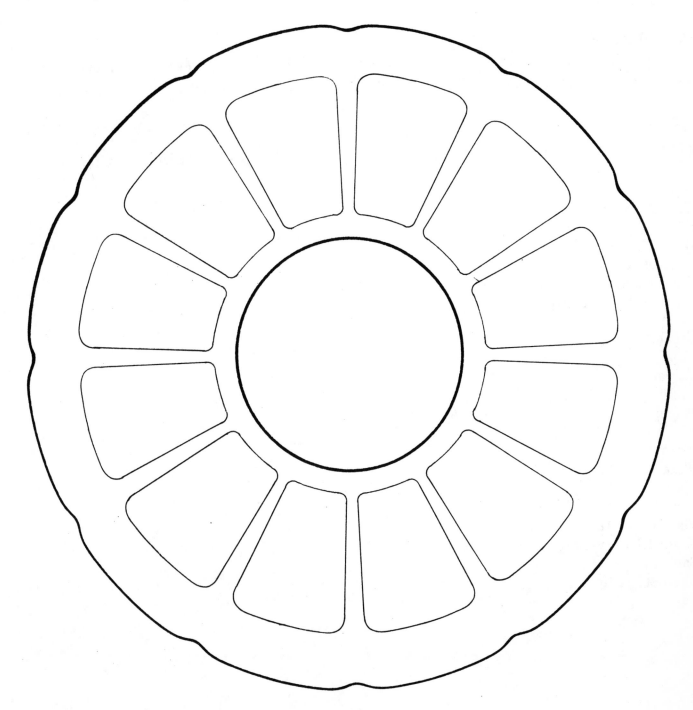

Colors found to date:

- Amber
- Green
- Black
- *Blue (Cobalt)
- Pink

*Too unique to price. No trade data found.

Reproductions or Reissues
None known to date.

General Pattern Notes
The blue pieces are very hard to come by. There have been a few pieces found that were elaborately decorated in gold, and some vessels have gold rims.

ITEM	DESCRIPTION & REMARKS	DOLLAR VALUE RANGES BY COLOR	
		Amber	Green or Pink
Bowl	6½"	12-14	8-11
Bowl	8½"	13-20	13-18
Bowl	9" (oval)	30-40	22-28
Bowl, Console	12"	36-46	22-28
Candlesticks	3" (pair)	33-40	20-26
Cheese and Cracker Set	12" (indented plate and a compote)	—	26-34
Compote	6"	17-21	13-16
Creamer		14-18	9-13
Cup		7-10	6-9
Goblet	5"	26-35	19-24
Gravy Boat	(with drip plate)	132-152	114-134
Mayonnaise Set	3½" (includes 8½" indented plate with a ladle)	48-63	33-41
Plate	6"	5-7	3-6
Plate	7"	8-10	4-8
Plate	8"	7-10	6-8
Plate	9"	14-16	9-14
Platter	12"	30-40	21-28
Sandwich Server	(center handled)	48-60	21-28
Saucer		6-9	3-6
Sherbet	(footed)	13-18	11-16
Sugar		13-18	10-12

WATERFORD

1938 - 1944, 1950's

Hocking Glass Company

(now Anchor-Hocking Glass Corporation)

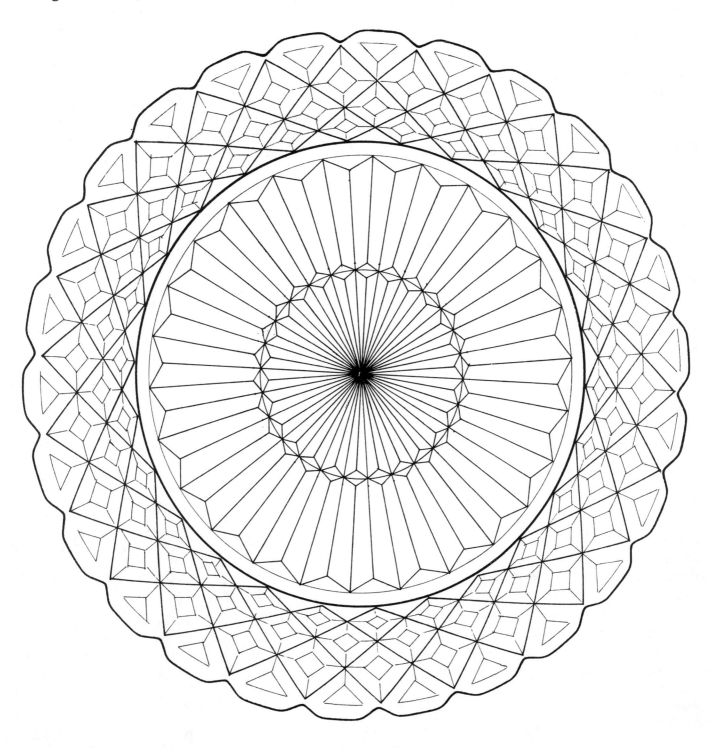

Colors found to date:

- Crystal
- *White (Opaque)
- *Green
- *Yellow
- Pink

*Items in this color only occasionally turn up. No trade data, so no values can be realistically assigned to them.

WATERFORD

Reproductions or Reissues

In the mid and late 1950's the company modified the old 13½-inch sandwich plate and produced a relish set. It consisted of a five-section plate with a small cup-like dish to be placed in the center, surrounded by inserts made in colors contrasting with the plate; red inserts with crystal and ivory inserts with a green plate. In addition, they released the 5¼-inch goblet in crystal.

General Pattern Notes

Once called "Waffle", this pattern was first produced by Hocking in 1938 in pink and phased out rather quickly, offering only occasional pieces in pink. Then the following year they introduced a full line of tablewear in crystal and added accessory pieces through the years until 1944. The green, white and yellow pieces may have been color experiments or whims of factory workers. In any case they are not found often.

ITEM	DESCRIPTION & REMARKS	DOLLAR VALUE RANGES BY COLOR	
		Crystal	Pink
Ash Tray		3-6	9-10
Bowl	4¾"	4-8	9-10
Bowl	5½"	10-11	15-19
Bowl	8¼"	10-11	15-19
Butter Dish and cover		26-32	209-264
Coaster	4"	2-5	5-9
Creamer	(oval)	3-6	11-14
Cup		4-8	13-18
Goblet	5¼"	13-14	—
Goblet	5 5/8"	24-30	—
Lamp	4" (rounded base)	33-42	—
Pitcher	42 oz. (tilted)	21-26	—
Pitcher	80 oz. (tilted)	33-42	121-151
Plate	6"	2-5	4-8
Plate	7 1/8"	3-6	4-8
Plate	9 5/8"	5-9	13-15
Plate, Cake 10¼" (handled)		5-9	13-15
Plate, Sandwich 13¾"		5-9	11-14
Relish	13¾" (5-sectioned)	20-24	—
Salt and Pepper (2 styles)		11-14	—
Saucer		1-4	4-8
Sherbet	(footed, 2 styles)	3-6	10-12
Sugar and cover		7-10	24-28
Tumbler	3½"	—	31-35
Tumbler	4 7/8" (footed)	10-12	13-18
Vase	6¾"	13-15	—

WINDSOR

1936 - 1946

Jeannette Glass Company

Jeannette, Pennsylvania

Colors found to date:

- Crystal
- Pink
- Delphite
- Red
- Green

WINDSOR

Reproductions or Reissues

None known to date.

General Pattern Notes

When Windsor was first released in 1936 it was a large line and only made in pink and green. In 1937 they apparently stopped production of the green and added crystal. That would explain the shortage of green items.

Candle holders are hard to find in pink.

An unusual boat-shaped (pointed at each end) bowl was produced but it is not remarkably priced. Nice to have in any collection of Windsor.

The delphite and red pieces turn up very infrequently. There has been insufficient trade data to establish realistic values for these colors.

ITEM	DESCRIPTION & REMARKS	DOLLAR VALUE RANGES BY COLOR		
		Crystal	Green	Pink
Ash Tray	5¾"	20-24	60-75	42-48
Bowl	4¾"	2-5	8-11	6-8
Bowl	5"	—	—	10-12
Bowl	5" (cream soup)	8-11	21-23	14-18
Bowl	5 1/8"	4-8	14-18	13-16
Bowl	5 3/8"	4-8	15-19	15-19
Bowl	7 1/8" (3-legged)	5-8	—	20-23
Bowl	8"	—	—	22-28
Bowl	8" (2-handled)	8-11	20-22	13-16
Bowl	8½"	8-11	14-16	13-16
Bowl	9½" (oval)	9-10	20-22	14-18
Bowl	10½" (blunted points on scalloped edge)	9-10	—	—
Bowl	10½" (sharp points on scalloped edge)	—	—	97-112
Bowl, Console 12½"		14-16	—	73-88
Bowl	7" x 11¾" (boat shaped)	14-18	28-36	26-32
Butter Dish		31-36	100-117	48-57
Cake Plate 10¾" (footed)		9-10	20-22	14-16
Cake Plate 13½"		9-10	14-19	14-16
Candlesticks 3" (pair)		20-22	—	71-87
Candy Jar and Cover		12-14	—	26-32
Coaster 3¼"		3-6	—	8-11
Compote		4-7	—	12-14
Creamer	(2 styles)	4-7	12-15	10-13
Cup		4-7	8-10	6-9
Pitcher	4½"	26-33	—	108-118
Pitcher	5"	9-10	—	—
Pitcher	6¾"	14-18	64-76	26-33
Plate	6"	2-6	4-8	3-7
Plate	7"	3-6	13-16	12-14
Plate	9"	3-6	13-16	11-14
Plate, Sandwich 10¼" (handled)		4-7	13-16	12-14
Plate	13 5/8" (salver)	11-13	19-24	19-23

ITEM	DESCRIPTION & REMARKS	DOLLAR VALUE RANGES BY COLOR		
Plate	15½"	9-10	—	—
Platter	11½" (oval)	6-8	13-16	12-14
Relish Platter	11½" (sectioned)	9-10	13-16	83-90
Salt and Pepper	(pair)	19-22	48-58	33-42
Saucer		2-5	4-8	3-6
Sherbet	(footed)	4-7	10-14	9-10
Sugar and cover	(3 styles)	7-11	22-29	19-24
Tray	4" (square)	2-5	10-13	6-10
Tray	4 1/8" x 9"	4-7	10-14	10-12
Tray	8½"' x 9¾" (handled)	8-10	27-33	26-33
Tray	8½" x 9¾" (without handles)	—	—	71-87
Tumbler	3¼"	4-7	13-18	13-16
Tumbler	4"	8-11	13-18	12-14
Tumbler	5"	8-11	27-33	19-23
Tumbler	4" (footed)	8-11	—	—
Tumbler	7¼" (footed)	10-11	—	—